The Voice Actor's Guide to HOME RECORDING

A money- and time-saving non-technical guide to making your own voiceover demos and auditioning from home or on location

by Jeffrey P. Fisher
and
Harlan Hogan

THOMSON

COURSE TECHNOLOGY
Professional ■ Trade ■ Reference

Front cover AT3060 image courtesy of Audio-Technica U.S., Inc.
Back cover Spike image courtesy of Mackie Technology.

SVP, Thomson Course Technology PTR: Andy Shafran
Publisher: Stacy L. Hiquet
Executive Editor: Mike Lawson
Senior Marketing Manager: Sarah O'Donnell
Marketing Manager: Heather Hurley
Manager of Editorial Services: Heather Talbot
Senior Editor: Mark Garvey
Associate Marketing Manager: Kristin Eisenzopf
Marketing Coordinator: Jordan Casey
Project Editor/Copy Editor: Cathleen D. Snyder
PTR Editorial Services Coordinator: Elizabeth Furbish
Interior Layout Tech: Stephen Ramirez
Cover Designer: Stephen Ramirez
Indexer: Sharon Shock
Proofreader: Tonya Cupp

ISBN: 1-93114-043-X
Library of Congress Catalog Card Number: 2004195188

Printed in the United States of America
05 06 07 08 DR 10 9 8 7 6 5 4 3 2 1

Thomson Course Technology PTR, a division of Thomson Course Technology
25 Thomson Place
Boston, MA 02210
http://www.courseptr.com

For Brian Holmsten:
Your friendship all these years has meant so much to me. Thanks!
—JPF

For Robert Phillips, John Jones, Rolf Brandis, John Ficca, and all the other great teachers
I've encountered. They penetrated my cranium—like WD-40 on a rusty hinge—and showed me
it was possible for a terminally shy kid to one day become a professional actor.
—H2

Acknowledgments

Harlan and Jeffrey would like to thank Mike Lawson, executive editor extraordinaire, for bravely seeing the need for this book. Also, our sincerest gratitude goes to Cathleen Snyder for her masterful job editing this text and for laughing at our all-too-often lame jokes. In addition, we'd like to thank our wives and children for putting up with us—always (not just when we write).

Jeffrey would also like to thank Harlan—the best writing partner a person could ever have. It was an absolute pleasure to work on this together! Harlan would like to point out, for the record, that he said equally nice things about Jeffrey as a friend and writing partner, but editor Cathleen has deleted them, citing: "Redundant!"

About the Authors

Jeffrey P. Fisher provides audio, video, music, writing, training, and media production services. He also teaches audio and video production at the College of DuPage in Glen Ellyn, Illinois, and writes extensively about music, sound, and video for print and the Web. He is the author of eight books, including *Instant Sound Forge*, *Moneymaking Music*, *Ruthless Self-Promotion in the Music Industry*, and *Profiting from Your Music and Sound Project Studio*.

Harlan Hogan is one of the most sought-after voiceover actors in the country. During his 30 years in the business, he has given voice to some of the most recognizable campaigns in advertising, including, "It's the cereal even Mikey likes," "That little itch should be telling you something," "Good things come to those who wait," and even "Hey, Culligan Man!" He's also heard on countless documentaries, and is that familiar voice that says, "This program was made possible by contributions to your PBS station from viewers like you. Thank you."

Based in North Barrington, Illinois, Harlan telecommutes via his own digital home studio, U-47 microphone, and ISDN Telos Zephyr. He is the writer of more than 50 radio and television commercials, more than 25 corporate and educational videos, three plays, and a book, *VO: Tales and Techniques of a Voiceover Actor*.

Contents

Acknowledgments IV

About the Authors V

Introduction IX

Chapter 1   **Shakespeare Would Have If He Could Have** 1

The Business of Getting Business: Auditions 4

The Business of Getting Business: Voice Demos 6

The Business of Getting Business: The Internet 7

The Business of Getting Business: Making Money Recording at Home 8

Talking the Talk: Studio Speak 8

Chapter 2   **Choosing a Computer for Home Recording** 9

Hardware Issues 11

Software 13

Internet Connection 14

Chapter 3   **Putting Together a Studio of Your Own** 17

Recording Overview 17

Microphones 19

Microphone Preamps 27

Digital Recording Software 30

Other Gear You Must Have 32

Setting Up the Room 34

Building a Recording Booth 38

Building a Different Recording Booth 39

Building a VO Box 39

Don't Be Shy: Ask for Help 41

Chapter 4   **Basic Production Procedures** 42

Setting Levels outside the Box 44

Setting Levels inside the Box 47

Spying Good Levels Onscreen 52

Getting Serious with the Microphone 55

Keep on Tracking 58

Get Set to Edit 63

Every Breath You Take 66

Editing on Your Computer 66

Chapter 5   **Long-Distance Direction: All about Phone Patches and ISDN** 70

Phone Patches 70

ISDN Patches 75

The Future on the Net? 80

Always Drop Both Lines! 81

Chapter 6   **Painless Promotion** 83

Making Your Own (or another Actor's) Killer Voice Demo 85

No Content? No Problem 87

How Long Should a Great Voice Demo Be? 88

All about Home Studio Auditions 89

Promoting Your New Facilities to Clients 90

Promoting Your New Facilities and Abilities to Other Actors   93

Expert Help 94

Home Studio, Legal, and Logistic Concerns 95

Now You've Built It and They Will Come! 96

Chapter 7   **Untangling the World Wide Web** 97

The Internet and the Voiceover Actor: A Practically Perfect Love Story 97

Audio Sites 99

A Domain of Your Own 100

Dedicated Web Hosting 101

Do-It-Yourself Web Design 103

Professional Web Design 105

Getting Your Voice Web-Ready 108

Preparing Your Files for Encoding 110

Virtual Voiceover 115

Chapter 8   **Advanced Techniques** 117

Got This Problem? 117

Adding Some Pizzazz 132

Adding Music and Sound Effects 134

Contents }

Multitracking 138
Finishing Secrets 141
Burn Baby Burn 141

Chapter 9   **Dénouement: Our Last Act** 146

Join Us Online 150

Appendix   **Resources** 152

Index 160

Introduction

Acting is the sweetest addiction…but how you gonna pay the rent?

Nightmare on West Meadowlark Lane

STAGE LIGHTS FADE UP ON THE PERFECTLY MODERN, PERFECTLY DECORATED, PERFECTLY EXPENSIVE KITCHEN OF GRIFF AND BETTE SMERSKY. GRIFF, IN BROOKS BROTHERS BUSINESS CASUAL, PERUSES THE WALL STREET JOURNAL AS JOHN, AGE 18, BURSTS THROUGH THE SWINGING DOORS STAGE RIGHT. IT IS MORNING.

John: Dad! I got in! I can't believe it….

Griff: I knew you would, Son.

              (HE HAS NOT LOOKED UP FROM THE PAPER.)

John: You did? Then it's okay?

Griff: It's more than okay, Johnny….

              (HE PEERS OVER THE TOP OF THE PAPER.)

Griff: (Continued) Sorry, I guess now that you're an official adult, I should make that John…. Anyway, I was so sure you'd make it I got you this….

              (GRIFF PULLS A HARVARD LAW SCHOOL SWEATSHIRT FROM BEHIND THE PAPER.)

John: Dad, I had an ACT score of 16….

Griff: (Broad grin) Right!

John: I flunked sophomore chemistry….

Griff: Right!

John: Second semester remedial Spanish…

Griff: Right!

John: And…

(TANNED, TERRIFIC, AND CLAD IN TOREADOR PANTS, BETTE ENTERS AND WIPES A SMUDGE OFF THE STAINLESS STEEL SIDE-BY-SIDE REFRIGERATOR.)

Bette: (Laughing) …don't forget Geometry for dummies. Oh, and that little incident last month—I don't know how much that cost your father….

Griff: (Laughing) Right!

John: So, Harvard Law?

Bette: Honey…

(SHE WIPES A SMUDGE FROM JOHN'S FACE AND STARTS TOWARD GRIFF, WHO GIVES HER A WITHERING LOOK. SHE CONTINUES STAGE LEFT TO POLISH THE STAINLESS STEEL DISHWASHER.)

Bette: (Continued) …we just don't know anyone at Princeton….

John: That's not my point; I don't want to go Harvard Law school.

Griff: Don't even say such a thing….

Bette: OHMYGOD!

John: (Holds up letter) I want to be an actor.

(BETTE SWOONS AGAINST THE HAND-CARVED GRANITE COUNTERTOP.)

Griff: Now look what you've done.

Bette: (Croaks out her line.) Griff, call Rudy. Tell him I cannot work out today or for the foreseeable future. We…we have a family crisis.

Griff: All the money I've spent, all the favors I've called in, and you want to major in basket weaving!

John: Acting!

Griff: Equally remunerative….

(BETTE CROSSES UPSTAGE, STEADIES HERSELF AT THE STAINLESS STEEL COMMERCIAL STOVE, AND THEN LUNGES FOR THE REFRIG-ERATOR AND PULLS AN EVIAN BOTTLE FROM WITHIN. SHE GULPS A SWIG WHILE CROSSING DOWNSTAGE AND TOSSES IT TO GRIFF, WHO SNATCHES IT FROM THE AIR WITH ONE HAND. BETTE CRADLES JOHN'S HEAD BETWEEN HER HANDS.)

Bette: Johnny, I've given up a perfectly good year of doubles tennis with the Macintoshes to slave over—golf! Honestly, it's croquet disguised as a…

(SHE LAUGHS HAUGHTILY.)

Bette: (Continued)…sport. And why? For you, darling. I've worn my triceps to the bone sucking up to Mr. and Mrs. Fat…the Albertsons, who happen to be the biggest—and not only in size—alumni contributors to Harvard Law! And now you want…you want…

John: (in Shakespearean style) To be…

Griff: An actor!

**Griff and
Bette:** How are you going to make a living?

Hi. This is Harlan Hogan. Remember when you told your parents you wanted to be an actor? I do. Our kitchen was nothing like the Smerskys', of course. I nervously sat at our tiny, yellow Formica and chrome table with my mom and my dad, a steelworker, and mustered up the courage to break the news. Truthfully, they were pretty supportive. But, like the fictitious Smerskys, they did (simultaneously as I recall) ask the same harrowing question, "How are you going to make a living?"

The fact is, it's a damn good question and assuming you haven't become (or aren't counting on becoming) an overnight sensation, it's a question with which you've already grappled. Acting is addictive, particularly theatre, but even Broadway barely pays a livable wage. Somewhere along the line you have to find ways to supplement your income. Waiting tables and working temp jobs is practically a tradition with modern thespians. But others actors, like myself, discovered there was a better way to use our acting skills and also pay the rent—voiceover work.

Personally, I've grown to enjoy voiceover performing so much that the theatre has been relegated to a supplemental job, rather than the other way around. Performing on camera in commercials, films, and videos helps actors pay the rent, of course, but nothing gives a return on your invested time like voiceovers.

Whether you are new to voiceover work or an experienced pro, you know how competitive and difficult it can be to carve out a successful voice-acting career. There are a number of books, classes, and coaches that can help, many of which we've listed in the "Resources" appendix. However, in this book we'll assume you already have some experience doing voiceovers and that now you want to expand your opportunities and income by setting up a home recording facility.

Why? Because as businesspeople would say, the voiceover paradigm has changed. New technology makes it imperative that we set up our own home studios not to compete with existing commercial recording studios, but to compete with other voice actors around the globe who have already embraced the wonders of ISDN and the Internet and are sending their auditions and finished voice tracks directly to producers. Becoming capable of recording yourself at home (or on location) also allows you not to miss voice auditions and sessions just because you're out of town, on location, or unwilling to arm-wrestle your way through bumper-to-bumper traffic and spend 20 bucks to park, just to read a 60-second audition in your agent's office. With in-house facilities you'll read it and e-mail it. It's that simple and efficient.

This book is all about setting up an affordable personal recording studio and learning how to use it so you can continue to be competitive despite the new paradigm we face as voiceover performers.

By this point I've managed to work the sexy, trendy term "paradigm" into my introductory section. Let's see how my co-author, professional recording engineer Jeffrey Fisher, sees this new paradigm from his perspective. You've no doubt noticed the term "paradigm" has passed my lips four times now without me breaking a sweat, so Jeffrey, the gauntlet—as Dubya Shakespeare might say—has been tossed, dropped, and thrown into your court.

Thanks—I think—Harlan. I'm Jeffrey Fisher, and when it comes to commercial work—radio, TV, films, documentary, and so on—time was and always will be money, no matter how the paradigm might change. Spending less time means spending less money. I know that's no great revelation, but more than ever, the need for speed permeates today's creative endeavors. It's all about shortened production and post-production schedules. Who can do the best work the fastest? That's the battle cry of purse-string-holding producers everywhere.

Simultaneously, producers and directors have become more technologically savvy. Although they might not know RAM from…uh…a ram, they do know that computers and other high-tech gear means things get done faster and better. And faster is cheaper. Better is always good, too.

Time compression and gee-whiz technology are real boons for the smart voice actor. How? Because you can make the work of an overloaded production team easier. If you can record yourself at home and e-mail back an audition almost instantly, or even record a real session, clean up your performance, and deliver a completed voice track in real time, you'll save the producer time and money, and you'll save yourself time and money, too! And for that, they'll reward you in some small way that usually involves cold, hard cash.

This book is about harnessing basic recording technology for your personal advantage. That's both good and bad. It's good in that you can use a simple recording setup to accomplish many tasks. It's bad in that you might be a technophobe, uncomfortable with all those knobs, switches, and cables. Oh, the cables. Geek spaghetti. I can hear you saying to yourself, "If this book is anything like my VCR instructions, I'm putting it back on the shelf."

Stop. Wait a minute. Whoa. Don't close the cover just yet. We can promise you that this book will help you dip your toes into the recording waters in a simple, no-nonsense way. And if you stick with us, you'll be swimming the recording ocean painlessly.

The truth is you can set up and run your own personal recording studio...and you will after reading this book! Otherwise, you'll never fully realize the potential you have using your voice, acting skills, a microphone, and a computer-based recorder. I promise the knobs will be few, the cables minimal, and the geek factor minimized to a few asides for the truly needy.

I've had the opportunity to work alongside novices and pros alike. I've also had the opportunity to teach novices and pros. What I've discovered is that those who aren't afraid of technology—those who are willing to take some chances and explore—are far more successful. People whose usually unfounded phobias paralyze them rarely seize the best opportunities. They get frustrated and ultimately fail. That's not you, right?

As one Neanderthal said millions of years ago, "Technology good, no be scared of new paradigm." Don't you be afraid, either. Technology and computers can make your life easier. They can frustrate you, but only if you let them. Technology is good when it works for you. It's part of your job to grab the new paradigm by its fluffy little ears and make it work for you. Don't be afraid of the computer or its peripherals. (Geek alert: Peripherals equals stuff you connect to the computer.) Treat your computer like the idiot savant it is and make it do what you ask—it will gleefully deliver (give or take a hiccup or two now and again).

Meanwhile, maybe little Johnny Smersky should have explained to his doting parents that by doing voiceover work, especially from home, the acting paradigm has changed.

Even Steven for the use of "paradigm," but notice, gentle reader, how my use of the term was always salient and meaningful, as opposed to you-know-who's....

Griff and Bette:	An actor! How are you going to make a living?
John:	With my mouth!
Bette:	Oh thank God, then you do want to be a lawyer!
John:	Whatever, Mom…

1 } Shakespeare Would Have If He Could Have…

Watching Tom Stoppard and Marc Norman's wonderful *Shakespeare in Love*, it was hard not to laugh at the sight of the bard's perpetually ink-stained hands, the inevitable result of having to laboriously write every wonderful word of prose and poetry with a quill. He was, like us, at the mercy of the technology of the times. Today, we're writing this book with our word processors, hands spotless. (Well, relatively—one of us did have some great ribs for dinner tonight, slow-cooked on the Weber grill, so there's a touch of sauce under someone's third fingernail on his left hand.)

Regardless, were the bard alive today, it's impossible to believe that he'd eschew our computer technology and continue to court the muse with pointed goose feather and drippy ink well. Although Jeffrey firmly believes he'd still wear that fabulous poofy-sleeved shirt.

If Bill—Harlan prefers Bill, Jeffrey prefers Will—were creating today, he'd be fluently up to his armpits in Word, WordPerfect, Final Draft, or even Movie Magic Screenwriter Convenience and cleanliness aside, computer-based word processing is the great "what if" machine. Let's say Bill typed, "I've got a question, to be or not to be?" and then thought better of the phrase. Well, he'd just cut, paste, and delete by highlighting the phrase "I've got a question," cutting it out of the beginning of the sentence, pasting it at the end, deleting "I've got a," and inserting "that is." So this line:

I've got a question, to be or not to be…?

would become this:

To be or not to be, that is the question....

More than likely, you are familiar with using software to accomplish the same type of word juggling. This is exactly how you'll soon be editing your own computer-based recordings. The basic skills are really that simple. In fact, a very experienced audio engineer told us recently, "The biggest change in editing audio isn't the elimination of tape and razor blades, it's that editing audio is now a visual skill. You see the audio (waveforms) on the screen and manipulate it the way you do text."

On a computer-based recording program Will's (okay, we've settled on calling him "Will" now...) first draft line looks like this:

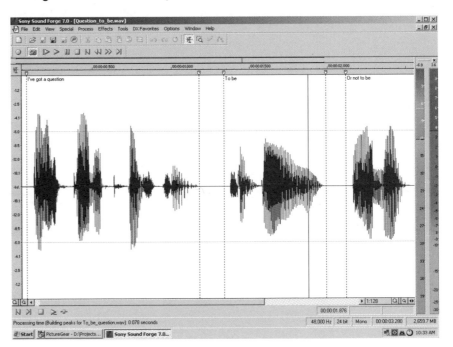

A bit of cut and paste later, it becomes the classic "To be or not to be:"

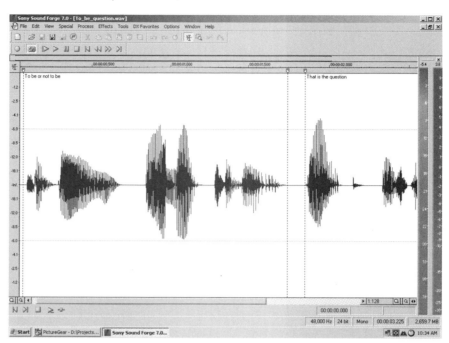

We'll assume throughout this book that you have some basic computer skills. If not, then set this book aside and, as Shakespeare might say, "Get thee to a computer class." You don't need to be an expert, but at least understand the fundamentals of opening and saving files, navigating, selecting, copying, cutting, pasting, using the mouse, using the Internet, and so on.

If the thought of setting up a studio and suddenly becoming a recording engineer intimidates you, relax. We'll show you the basic skills you need to survive in a new world. More than likely, you'll find recording and editing a lot of fun. Remember, these new skills are just as important to you, an actor in the twenty-first century seeking voiceover work, as is your training in movement, makeup, improvisation, and voice. Nothing stands still in the creative world, and those who refuse to learn new skills generally get left behind.

Or, as in the words of Will's lesser-known cousin's sister's nephew's twice-removed next-door neighbor, "Poop, or get thou off thy pot."

❄ ❄ ❄

The Business of Getting Business: Auditions

Performing and making money doing voiceovers starts with the biggest challenge an actor faces—getting the work. Even the most established and successful voiceover actors audition. A lot. But auditioning is costly in both time and money.

MY LUNCH WITH HARLAN
A very, very independent film

FADE IN:

INT:

CROWDED RESTAURANT. JEFFREY SITS AT A TABLE NEAR THE BACK, GLANCES AT CLOCK. HARLAN ENTERS RUNNING, SPOTS HIM, AND GRABS A SEAT OPPOSITE HIM.

Jeffrey: You look beat.

Harlan: I'm late, sorry. I had three scripts to read at Stewart, then ran over to Audio Recording Unlimited for a VOX Chicago audition, then got the car out of hock and drove to O'Connor Casting for a mind-numbing cattle call. Don't get me wrong Jeffrey, I'm grateful to be included but I gotta tell ya, I've spent over twenty bucks on just parking today, and I don't get paid for auditions.

Jeffrey: Ah, the actor's lament.

Harlan: True, but if we don't audition, we don't get cast. No sessions, no money, no lunch with wealthy recording engineer friends….

Jeffrey: You're right….

Harlan: Glad you agree….

Jeffrey: …about lunch, I'm ignoring the wealthy dig. Let's order 'cuz I think the waitress is in a hurry. She's been giving me the "shut up and order" look.

ECU: HARLAN FRANTICALLY SCANNING MENU

CUT TO: POV JEFFREY

Jeffrey: So why don't you just record your own auditions and e-mail yourself around town, or across the country? Your agent generally does that with the tracks you record there anyway, doesn't she?

ANGLE ON: TABLE

Harlan: Yeah, they convert everything to MP3 files and send 'em off but...

Jeffrey: So, set up a simple recording studio at your place and do your auditions in your underwear.

ANGLE ON: HARLAN

Harlan: That would be a brief session, then?

Jeffrey: A genuine skivvies session...

FULL SHOT: WAITRESS ENTERS

Harlan: Ah, but what to choose...boxers or briefs? Boxers or briefs, that is the question...whether 'tis nobler to...

Waitress: C'mon fellas, let's order up. I've got an audition to get to....

FADE OUT:

THE END

All across the country, auditioning voice scripts from home-based studios is becoming the norm, not the exception. In England, approximately 90 percent of actual recording sessions are done via digital phone lines from voice actors' homes—not just auditions. Auditioning and recording using home studios is truly a win-win proposition for everyone involved—actors, casting agents, talent agents, and producers. Aside from the obvious convenience, it means you no longer have to miss out on important auditions or sessions because you are out of town on vacation or hopefully on location shooting a major film. You can take the same skills and much of the same equipment you use in your home studio on the road, so you can e-mail your tracks to and from anywhere.

For actual sessions (and for some auditions), a producer will want to direct you so you'll use the good old-fashioned telephone for a "phone patch," or you might use a high-tech digital ISDN digital telephone system. The fact is, more and more producers simply expect voice talent to have professional-quality home studios. That way, they can get the performer they want without worrying about where the talent is physically located, and without the hassle and considerable costs of booking two separate recording studios. Some clients—the ones we all love—are actually willing to pay you an additional fee for the use of your studio!

If you want to do promo work for radio and TV stations, you'll have to have ready access to a studio with at least a high-speed Internet connection, but preferably one with ISDN capability. By the way, when you find yourself recording nationally and internationally, you just might have to brush up on those world time zones you never bothered to learn back in middle school.

The Business of Getting Business: Voice Demos

In the voiceover world, you need a top-notch voice demo, and you must keep that demo up to date. But the cost of producing and constantly revising a voice demo seems to escalate as fast as the home prices in Marin County. This is another area where your home-based recording studio can save you money and keep you competitive. You might even find your home studio actually makes you money.

The most expensive part of producing voice demos is that daunting "what if" phase. You assemble all the audio clips from your recent work or pay for studio time to record "created" tracks and assemble them into a couple of minutes of dynamite audio. After paying a hefty studio bill, you play your new masterpiece for your agent or a producer or two, and guess what? It's back to the studio to cut and paste, moving this spot there, re-recording that one, lowering the sound effects on the movie trailer, tightening up the narration section, and eliminating the middle spot that your agent said, as pleasantly as possible, "just sucks."

This ongoing process makes the bills stack up and, just like going to auditions, the expense comes out of your pocket because that perfect demo isn't creating any business—yet. Finally you're finished, dupes are ordered, and then you land a major network commercial, one that you and your agent agree you just *have* to have on your demo. So it's back to the studio to do it all over again.

Your home studio can save you thousands during this assembly period. You can record spec spots to your heart's content, working for the perfect take. You can assemble the first draft, what engineers call the *rough-cut*, to play for your agent, and re-cut and re-mix it over and over with nary a bill in the mailbox from your favorite studio. When you are happy (okay, when you are 99 percent happy, because no voice actor is ever 100 percent content with his or her demo), you can take your audio files to a professional recording engineer to sweeten them and make the final version for duplication. Don't skip this step; the little you'll pay for his or her professional expertise is invaluable to the final product. You just might find the demo assembly process so interesting that you'll want to begin producing and recording demos for other actors, for a modest fee and a nice return on your recording equipment investment.

The Business of Getting Business: The Internet

The Internet is not only your electronic post office for sending your voice coast to coast, it's an even better way to showcase your voice talent than traditional media, such as CDs. As any voiceover artist from newbie to old pro knows, the expense of designing, duplicating, and distributing your voice demos once you've got them perfected can be astronomical. One top Midwest talent recently sent out 12,000 CDs of his work! Postage costs alone are staggering, not to mention the packing envelopes, CD cases, labels, and cover art.

The Web offers a better, more cost-effective way to make your demos available to prospective employers. The expense of maintaining a basic Web site is marginal compared to traditional distribution. With your home recording studio you can change, update, and customize your voice demos as often as you want and post them on your personal Web page, as well as your agent's site or other Web-based voiceover sites with which you might be affiliated.

The Business of Getting Business: Making Money Recording at Home

In addition to possibly recording and assembling demos for other actors, you might find that your little recording rig, engineering skills, and acting talent can earn you even more extra money. You could handle the audio load for many lower-budget productions including radio spots, on-hold messages, or even video soundtracks. And you might branch out into other audio-related areas, such as music and sound design—a fancy name for sound effects.

Talking the Talk: Studio Speak

If you've ever taken up a new hobby or sport, probably the hardest part was learning the language so you could "talk the talk." You can learn the basics of sailing in an hour of so, but you might spend a lifetime learning all the lingo. Halyards, vangs, and mainsheets are incomprehensible terms to a landlubber. While actors wax poetic on the subtle nuances taught by Stanislavski, Boleslawsky, Strasberg, and Meisner, they often find themselves flummoxed by the seemingly arcane terms tossed around in the recording studio. (Jeffrey can, however, guarantee that no recording engineer would ever use the word "flummoxed" in a conversation.) From compression ratios to decibels and waveforms—the non-sailing kind—we promise we'll demystify the nomenclature so you can talk the talk that pays the bills while you get on with the fun part: recording, editing, and mixing your own audio.

We're confident Will Shakespeare would agree. "A studio of your own? Now that is the answer!"

2 } Choosing a Computer for Home Recording

You need a recording device that captures your spoken word performance. Cassettes are out and mini-discs passé. There are other stand-alone digital recorders available today that are all-in-one boxes including microphone inputs, preamps, recorder, and more. These devices work fine, but they lack other flexibility that a computer brings to you. They can't do word processing, connect to the Internet, or let you play Mah Jongg or Backgammon in your spare time, so we suggest you avoid these boxes.

Plain and simple: You need to get your voice into the computer for the following reasons:

▶ **Quality.** Digital recordings are far superior to almost any other format available today. They are low noise and they faithfully reproduce the sounds recorded.

▶ **Speed.** Working in the digital domain is fast and efficient. You can edit your sound recordings just like you edit a document in a word processor, and you can make your performances tighter and better.

▶ **Ease.** Most recording software today is fairly easy to set up and use. It works much like a familiar cassette deck, but with far more powerful features. And it sounds infinitely better than any cassette ever did!

▶ **Flexibility.** You can deliver your finished recordings on a CD or e-mail them to an agency or client. In short, a computer serves as the center of your voiceover empire. Not only can you record, edit, and deliver your voiceover work, you can use the computer for many other tasks, such as

Internet surfing, e-mailing, writing, promoting, bookkeeping, and so much more!

When it comes to computers, there are of course two choices: Macs and PCs. We're confident that the debate over which is better will continue forever. The point is, it really doesn't matter which platform you choose; it comes down to software. And the software you need to record is readily available for both PC and Mac environments. Although we'll feature PC-based software in this book, the basic concepts you learn will be completely applicable to any Mac-based software you choose.

So which computer should you buy? Our advice for grabbing the computer you need to record, edit, mix, and deliver your voice is really quite simple. Get the biggest and best you can afford! Get the fastest, biggest hard drive(s) and the most RAM you can for the money you have available. Any computer you buy new off the shelf will be more than adequate for voiceover recording; however, if you decide to edit digital *video*, you need something more robust. Toddle on down to your local computer superstore—CompUSA, Best Buy, Circuit City, and so on—or go online to Gateway or Dell and see what you can afford.

Watch for deals by the major computer vendors, too. They often run specials and package deals, including enticing payment options. Best Buy once offered an 18-month no-interest with payments option. For about $100 a month, you could get a really good system.

When selecting a computer system, first consider the software you will use. Which audio software do you like the most? The best way to find out is to get a demo version and start playing with it. Most audio software companies offer "dumbed-down" but fully operational downloads of their programs for free on the Internet. Once you've used the software for a few recordings, you should have a clear idea whether it's right for you. Ahhhh, but as Billy (we're all close enough to call him "Billy") Shakespeare might muse, "Here's the rub...how can thou test software without first owning a computer?" You could borrow a computer from a friend or relative, or go to your local library, cybercafe, or even Kinko's. There you can mess around with a Mac or PC to see which is right for you. Now, the library and other establishments won't be too excited about you adding software to their machines, but a friend or relative probably won't mind.

Key issues to consider when buying a computer are obviously the operating system "software" (Mac OS or Windows) and the hardware to run it and other software—the audio program, word processing application, accounting functionality, and so on. Currently, the Mac is running OS X and Windows is running XP, but this will change—you can bet on it! Most software packages follow the changes in operating systems, so compatibility usually isn't a problem.

Hardware Issues

The basic hardware in any computer system includes a computer *central processing unit* (CPU for short), a soundcard, monitor, keyboard, mouse, and probably a printer. The information in this section applies whether you choose a laptop or desktop model.

The computer CPU needs a decent hard drive, enough RAM to run your programs well, and a CD or CD/DVD writer. Stick to Pentium (P4s) or equivalent processors in the PC world and G4/G5 processors in the Mac domain. Watch out for the Centrino and Mobile laptop PCs because they often can't handle recording and playing back audio well enough. Get a large-capacity hard drive—40 GB or more—with fast access times. (GB = gigabytes = billions of bytes = a lot of storage space for voice recordings, pictures of your dog or cat, e-mails from friends, and other such stuff.) In fact, for audio and video, a second hard drive makes everything run smoother and faster. Your computer can use one drive just to store and use the recording program and the other to store and manipulate the audio you are recording. Like so many other electronic devices, the cost of hard drives has plummeted, so buy two—they're cheap!

You might see the hard drive referred to as a 7200 RPM drive. That's the perfect (fast) speed—7200 revolutions per minute. You'll want a big drive because audio files are rather large—10 MB/minute at CD-quality stereo. Record a 15-minute piece and you've used 150 MB of space. Delve into digital video, and the hard drive space necessary to work increases exponentially. Wow, we managed to use "delve" and "exponentially" in a single sentence!

RAM is the memory the computer needs to store programs, drivers, and other information. Again, more is better—256 MB is today's minimum, but

512 MB is better. Your audio programs will run substantially faster and with fewer problems if you install more RAM.

Although you'll most often be sending auditions as MP3s via the Internet, we still consider a CD or CD/DVD writer as another mandatory piece of equipment. Because audio files are so large, you need a distribution medium big enough to hold them, and CDs are perfect. The ability to burn CDs, either audio or data, means you can make demos at home, produce your audio projects, and then mail them to clients. And CDs can be used to inexpensively back up your work. Software to operate the CD or CD/DVD writer is usually included with the computer. Today, blank CDs cost just pennies, so while you're at the computer store pick up a spindle of blank CDs. You'll need them.

Every computer sold today comes equipped with a soundcard or audio interface of some kind. The problem is that most of them are completely unsuitable for serious sound recording. Laptop soundcards are particularly yucky. That said, with external gear (namely a better-quality mic and pre-amp, the subject of Chapter 3, "Putting Together a Studio of Your Own"), a basic soundcard could suffice in a pinch.

But (and this is a *big* but), we *highly* recommend you invest in an audio interface specifically designed to handle quality audio recording. Many come with their own cards that need to be installed in the computer. Yikes! Squeamish about the prospect of opening up the computer and putting something in it? Hire a pro to do it for you. Thankfully, newer models connect to the computer's USB or FireWire port, making it a snap to get up and running quickly. These connections are really simple—virtually plug and play—so don't worry about it. Chapter 3 includes a complete discussion about these devices.

The mouse and keyboard are included with every computer. However, there are a couple of extra pieces that can make recording and editing a little easier. One, the Keyspan Digital Media Remote (http://www.keyspan. com), is a wireless handheld TV/VCR-type remote for your computer. You'll often have to record and perform at the same time, and this handy little device lets you control your recording software remotely.

The Contour Design ShuttlePRO V2 (http://www.contourdesigns.com) gives you extra control over your digital recording software. The jog knob lets you move through your audio files with ease. Its 15 programmable buttons automate your most-used tasks. It's preprogrammed for most software titles, too. Use it along with a mouse to really speed up your work.

Computer monitors come in several flavors and sizes. It's much easier to work on 17" and 19" monitors, but they are desk hogs (and electrical hogs, too). The thin, energy-conscious LCD screens are beautiful, but at a high price, especially at larger sizes. Though LCD monitors are now common, the big 'uns are still pricey. So if you have tabletop room and are on a budget, you can score huge conventional monitors for pennies compared to the sexy thin models.

A color printer is another great idea. You can make fancy labels for your CDs, print scripts, and more. There are myriad choices for less than $150. Get one.

Software

Obviously, you'll need some recording software. We discuss this subject in excruciating detail in the next chapter. But what other software would be useful for a professional voice acting career?

Essential to almost any business is a solid word processor. You'll use it for everything—scripts, letters, promotions, résumés, and all the important information about every aspect of your career.

Some kind of contact management system, called a *PIM* or *Personal Information Manager*, is another good choice. You can use the information stored in its database to keep track of appointments, clients, and prospects, and to generate mailing lists easily for your ongoing promotions. Harlan uses ACT! and Jeffrey prefers a custom database he created himself. Harlan is clearly content to do without the whitewall tires, shiny red paint, and thundering exhaust pipes that feature prominently in Jeff's design. There is even a specific career management program called, appropriately enough, Actor Track (http://www.holdonlog.com). For around a hundred dollars, the software keeps track of auditions, sessions, callbacks, and more and it can interface with your PDA. What's a PDA? We thought you'd never ask. Read on, McDuff!

A Personal Digital Assistant (PDA), such as a Palm Pilot or a Blackberry, can really make your life easier. With its included address book, to-do lists, memos, and calendar, a PDA coupled with your computer is a one-two punch to keep you organized. It's even easier to keep track of people, appointments, deadlines, and more. Plus, synchronizing data between the computer and a handheld PDA is a snap. Once you use one, you'll never go back to the old ways of managing information. We guarantee it.

Accounting software targeted for the small business is another possible software purchase. Use it to keep track of personal and business income and expenses and manage all your financial affairs, including income tax preparation. Quicken and Microsoft Money are the leaders in this area.

Because you'll be burning CDs and perhaps DVDs, you might want a program that helps you design, lay out, and print labels, booklets, and tray cards. You can put together a top-notch demo package with this software and a color printer. If you're graphically challenged, skip this program and hire a real designer to put together your package.

Internet Connection

This next item is mandatory on your list of needs. Having a computer without an Internet connection is like having a toaster and no bread. Essentially, you need four key items—a way to access the Internet, an e-mail address, a Web domain, and space to hold your Web site. The last two items are the subject of Chapter 7, "Untangling the World Wide Web"; the first two are addressed here.

You need to be able to connect to the Internet and access its many functions. Signing up with any of the big service providers is all you need to do: Comcast, AOL, NetZero...the list goes on. You also need to choose the kind of connection you'll use. A dial-up connection uses a computer modem connected to your telephone line. Most computers have the necessary hardware for a dial-up connection. This method does tie up your phone, meaning you might miss an important call...like a booking! Also, a dial-up connection is very slow, which means sending large audio files, even compressed MP3s, can take a looooooooooooong time.

If you choose this route, consider at least getting a second phone line just for this connection or sharing it with a fax, and using your other phone line for its intended purpose of ordering pizzas and complaining to fellow actors how slow it is. If you really can't afford a second line, at least order voicemail from your phone company so people who call won't get a busy signal.

Faster connections include cable modems, DSL lines, and ISDN. These connections keep you connected to the Internet at all times and don't tie up your "talk" phone line. They are significantly faster than dial-up connections, but not surprisingly a bit more costly and not always available everywhere.

When you sign up with an Internet service, you'll get an e-mail address. Choose a user name that's easy to remember and avoid goofy, strange, incomprehensible, and otherwise bad choices. Studmuffin@suchnsuch.com is probably a wise choice if you're an idiot. 1$pxq&yzzzqf@suchnsuch.com is another great idea...if you never want anybody to ever remember your address or be able to type it correctly.

For good examples, see how our e-mail addresses are logical and easy to remember: harlan@harlanhogan.com and jpf@jeffreypfisher.com. Since domain names have become very inexpensive, consider buying variations on your name, especially if your name is commonly misspelled. Harlan owns harlanhogan.com, harlinhogan.com, harlandhogan.com, and harlenhogan.com, and he gets scads of hits on all these "wrong" spellings. And Jeffrey owns harlanisnothisrealname.com, but so far only collection agencies have clicked on that site. Today, you can also take advantage of "extensions" other than the ubiquitous ".com," such as .biz, .tv, .us, .net, and so on.

The Internet is a main ingredient in your recipe for success. Learn to use it to your best advantage—for research, to find sessions, to contact key people, to take care of personal and career matters, and so much more. If you've been living under a rock for the past few years and you know little about the Internet, go to the library or bookstore and get a few books on the subject, spend several afternoons with geeky friends paying rapt attention as they surf the Net, or swallow your pride and sign up for a course at the local community college or high school.

What you *can't* do is cop a plea, "Oh, I'm an actor and can't be troubled with revolutionary changes that affect the very foundations of society and communication." No go, kiddo—that is, not if you want to make a buck or two in the new world of voiceovers. Buying a computer can be a daunting task for the uninitiated. Thankfully, today you don't have to worry about buying the wrong system (or one that doesn't have enough power for what you need). We can't emphasize enough that any computer you buy today that meets or exceeds the specifications outlined in this chapter will work for you. Lesser models might also work, but why risk it?

Take this book with you to the store and talk to a knowledgeable seller. Explain what you will be doing with your computer and show the salesperson this chapter. Better still, take along a professional or a reasonably computer-literate person (it's geek time once again!) to hold your hand as you shop. And use your best acting skills to stay in the moment, thereby ignoring his or her horn-rimmed glasses—the ones permanently repaired with a safety pin.

3 } Putting Together a Studio of Your Own

For voice work, the basic recording equipment is quite simple: microphone, microphone preamplifier, and digital recorder. That's it. Well, almost…

With such a simple arrangement, you can clearly see how the quality of each link can greatly affect the sound you record. A crummy microphone hooked to the best computer will still sound like a crummy microphone. While you don't have to spend vast sums to get a good sound, you can't get by with bargain basement junk either. Investing wisely in the right components at this stage will pay off for you down the road.

Recording Overview

Warning: The following section contains material that falls into the category of "nice to know," not "need to know." We know from personal experience that a thorough knowledge of the arcane intricacies of how recording actually works will not make you more charming at parties.

It all starts with capturing the sound of your voice clearly, cleanly, and accurately while presenting your best performance in a recording. Sound is produced by something vibrating. In this case, vocal cords wiggling around in your throat produce your particular sound. The vibration transfers its energy to the air that moves from your lungs out through your mouth and nose.

You've probably heard sound described as waves, moving out in all directions like a stone dropped in a pond. Like a wave, sound energy has crests and troughs. At the sound wave's top, the air is compressed together tightly. At its trough, the air is loose. This is how sound energy travels through air; the air itself does not move. We call this *acoustic energy.*

To record the sound of your voice, you need to convert the acoustic energy into something that can be recorded. A microphone captures acoustic energy and converts it to electrical energy that is the same as or *analogous* to the original acoustic sound. This electrical energy from the microphone can be amplified and played through a speaker. A speaker is really a microphone in reverse, converting electrical energy back to acoustic energy that can then be heard by our ears.

Also, electrical energy can be converted to magnetic energy and recorded on tape. A magnet in the recorder arranges tiny grains of oxidized metal in a pattern that is once again analogous to the electrical energy from the microphone. It is from this analogous concept that we get the term *analog recording.* And now you know why recording tape looks a lot like Scotch tape with rust stuck on it—because that's pretty much what it is.

Digital recording converts the electrical energy into information the computer can understand. Computers only know two numbers: 0 and 1. By manipulating these ones and zeros, they do the tasks we assign. Digital sound recording uses an analog-to-digital converter (ADC) to convert electrical energy into ones and zeros through a process called *sampling.* The ADC is part of the computer's soundcard. Essentially, the computer takes an electronic snapshot of the electrical waveform moment by moment and assigns it numbers that represent the sound frozen in time.

For CD-quality sound, the computer's ADC takes 44,100 snapshots per second! That number, abbreviated as 44.1 kHz, is called the *sampling rate.* The higher the sampling rate, the better quality the digitized sound.

Once a computer takes a digital snapshot or sample, it needs to assign a value to the sound that represents its volume or amplitude. The *bit depth* determines the possible values available. CD quality uses 16 bits. Computers round or *quantize* all samples to one of those 65,536 possible values. As with sampling rate, the higher the bit depth, the better the sound.

Microphones

Okay, now that we've addled your brain with way too much information on how recording actually works, let's start putting together the components you'll need to get to work recording yourself at home or on location. As the first link in the recording chain, microphones are a critical component. Although it's possible to spend an arm, leg, and thigh on a good one, you'll be relieved to know that decent-quality mics can be bought for less than $100 with a myriad of even better choices between $200 and $400.

And what about that cute little microphone that came with your computer? It's garbage, and you certainly don't want to record your dulcet tones with garbage, do you? Throw it away. Right now. We'll wait.

With that nasty business over and done with, we can get down and dirty with microphones. There are essentially two types: dynamics and condensers. *Dynamic microphones* create their own electricity. How, you say? (Now don't deny it—Harlan and I distinctly heard you mutter, "Whaaaaaa?") Do you remember doing a science experiment where you lit a tiny light bulb by moving a magnet inside a coil of wire? No? Well, a magnet moving in a coil of wire is an electrical generator. From the turbines at the Hoover Dam to the most sophisticated nuclear power plant, we generate electricity by moving magnets in coils of wire, and that's precisely how—to answer your question—a dynamic makes its own electricity.

Inside a dynamic microphone there is also thin diaphragm that moves back and forth when struck by acoustic energy (for example, your voice). This diaphragm is attached to a coil of wire that moves over a strong magnet. The electrical energy that flows matches the sound wave. Dynamic mics are sometimes called *moving coil microphones*, but not by anybody we know.

A *condenser microphone* needs electricity to work properly. Once again a thin diaphragm, often made of gold foil, moves freely to the sound striking it. The diaphragm and a solid plate behind it have an electrical charge applied to them. The action of the diaphragm moving toward and away from the plate creates a varying electrical current that is analogous to the sound waveform. This tiny amount of electricity is then amplified and output from the microphone. Condensers get their power from batteries, separate power supplies, or the sound mixers they are plugged into on their way to the recorder.

❋ ❋ ❋

Dynamic mics are rugged and often less expensive. In fact, when Electro-Voice introduced the EV 666 dynamic mic back in the late '50s, salesmen would often tell broadcasters it was so sturdy that it could do double-duty as a hammer in the event that an announcer forgot to bring one along to a remote broadcast and he needed to pound in some ten-penny nails to hold up the station's call-letter banner! As you'd suspect, a big chunk of sound quality was traded for that kind of ruggedness. Condenser mics are fragile by comparison but they are perfect for picking up the subtleties of a sound. Large diaphragm condenser models are particularly well-suited for voice, sung or spoken.

How a microphone responds to sound is called its *pickup pattern*. There are three primary pickup patterns: omnidirectional, unidirectional or cardioid, and super-directional or shotgun. Another word of warning: Discussing these patterns with attractive strangers will not help your personal pickup pattern! *Omnidirectional microphones* pick up sound in all directions. Picture the mic in the middle of a transparent globe and you'll see how it responds to sound from all directions, including from behind what you might call the business end. Omni means "all," so the name omnidirectional is apt. The problem with omnis is they can hear all the background noises along with your voice. They are useful for things such as man-in-the-street interviews and some music situations, but voice recording is not their strong point.

Unidirectional or *cardioid microphones* are more sensitive in one direction and reject sounds coming from the rear. Picture a heart-shaped pattern and you'll see how it picks up sound. This heart-shaped pattern is why these mics are called cardioids, the prefix cardio meaning "heart." Cardioids are ideally suited to voice work because they focus on your voice and significantly reduce other background noises.

The *shotgun microphone* has an even tighter pickup pattern than a regular cardioid, letting you really zero in on the sound you want and reject the rest. Used heavily in the film industry to record on-camera dialogue, the shotgun is also a closely guarded secret in the voice recording world. A mini-shotgun, such as the Sennheiser 416, gives that tight, omniscient announcer quality so sought after for many radio and TV spots. It's not a cheap microphone, but its sound can really cut through. Guess who has one of those, too? (If you picked Harlan, give yourself 1,000 points.) (Oh yeah! Well, guess who paid about half the price of a brand-new 416 by shopping eBay?)

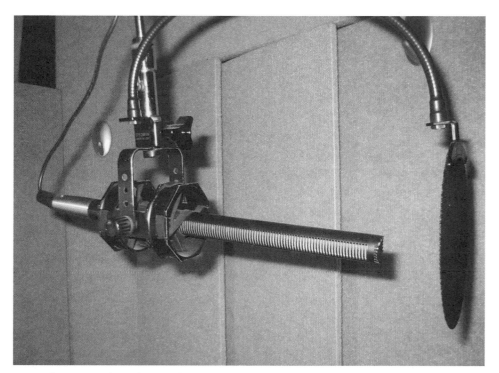

A mini-shotgun, such as the Sennheiser 416, works well for that announcer voice quality.

Cardioids and shotguns do suffer from a phenomenon called *proximity effect*, which is not the same as the feeling you get in an overcrowded elevator. As you get closer to cardoid and shotguns, the low frequencies or bass becomes pronounced. This can work to your advantage, making a thin voice sound deeper and fuller. Or it might work against you, depending on your vocal quality. If you need the bass boost, get closer to the mic. If not, back away a little until it sounds good.

Notice the Shure SM57 picks up sound from the top, but the Marshall 2001 picks up sound from the side. Make sure you know how your microphone works so you talk into the correct place.

Bringing Mics to the Table

Less than $150	Less than $400	Less than $1,000	Money to Burn
Audio-Technica AT2020	Audio-Technica AT3035	AKG C414	Neumann U87
Marshall MXL 990	Marshall MXL 2003	Audio-Technica AT3060	Neumann U47
Shure SM57 or SM58	Rode NT1-A	Electro-Voice RE20	
	Sennheiser MD 421	Neumann TLM 103	
	Shure KSM27	Sennheiser MKH416	
		Shure KSM44	

Shure SM57 or SM58 dynamic mics are ideal first choices for recording your voice (http://www.shure.com). They can be picked up for less than $100 and sound remarkably good on a variety of voices. Generally, the '57 is better suited to the male voice, while the '58 sings for females. However, your voice might be the exception to this rule, so if you can, record some tests and evaluate further before making a final buying decision.

At less than $300, the Sennheiser MD 421 is also a good dynamic choice (http://www.sennheiser.com). On the higher end, the Electro-Voice RE20 (around $700) is a mainstay in the radio world (http://www.electro-voice.com). This dynamic mic is known for its warm, fat FM-DJ sound.

The less expensive large-diaphragm condensers that permeate the market today do an even better job of capturing voice. On the low end, either the Marshall MXL 2001 or MXL 2003 (Jeffrey's favs) work quite well. And at less than $150 each, they're a bargain (http://www.mxlmics.com). The MXL 990 is another fine choice, and it is even cheaper (less than $100). The Rode NT1-A (http://www.rodemicrophones.com), Audio-Technica AT3035 (http://www.audio-technica.com), and Shure KSM27 are other choices for less than $300. For a little bit more, the Neumann TLM 103 (http://www.neumann.com) is a very popular mic for voice work and is reasonably affordable at less than a thousand dollars. You can find many mics at a considerable discount online and on eBay.

The high end brings the AKG C414 (http://www.akg-acoustics.com), Audio-Technica AT3060, Shure KSM44, and Neumann U87 (http://www.neumann.com). Many engineers agree the Neumann 87 and 89 are fantastic choices for voice recording...at a high price, though. Harlan has an old Neumann U47 microphone that dates back to pre-Beatles-era recording.

This baby is well-respected and much sought after, and depending on the model, it can fetch from $7,000 to as much as $15,000!

The Holy Grail of microphones

Choosing the right mic comes down to two issues—what sounds best for you and how much cold, hard cash you are willing to spend. If $100 is all you have, grab an SM57, SM58, or, better still, the MXL 990. If you have more money, consider testing a few mics at a local music store. The bigger stores—Guitar Center, Sam Ash, and Mars Music—are usually set up for microphone auditioning. Take a script in and record a few short tests. Play it back and evaluate the best choice for your voice. What should you listen for? You want your voice to sound natural with no strange artifacts (boominess, shrillness, Elliot Ness, or any other nesses).

Generally, males sound good on almost any large-diaphragm condenser. The same holds true for most female voices. However, some condensers are rather bright, and that can bring out excessive esses, called *sibilance*, in a female voice. Sibilance can really mar a good recording, so matching the right microphone to a female voice is often more critical than doing so with a male voice. The SM58 dynamic and Sennheiser 421 are less bright and may work better for female voices. Unfortunately, only testing the mics can determine the right choice for you. If you have an opportunity to try out a number of different mics at a recording studio and get some expert advice from the audio engineer, by all means jump at the chance.

So you've chosen a microphone. Don't forget to get a good-quality cable to hook it up to the next step in the recording chain. Professional mics are balanced, which makes them less susceptible to electrical noise (hum to you and me and even Harlan, who is, admittedly, tone deaf). Know how most modern electrical appliances wires have a third (ground) plug? Well, a balanced cable works pretty much the same way and has balanced XLR connections on each end. Get a cord long enough to reach from your recording area to your gear, but try to keep it as short as possible so you don't lose any sound quality. Also, get a microphone stand with a boom arm if you can. This makes positioning the microphone easier. You might want to get a desk stand instead of a boom/stand should you decide on the build the voice box idea. (See the "Building a VO Box" section later in this chapter.)

Many of the large condensers come with a special shock mount that holds the microphone on the stand. These web like contraptions effectively isolate the mic from picking up minor bumps and thumps. Use one!

Pop filters help prevent plosives from ruining your recordings.

Here's one more important accessory. Invest in a good pop screen to keep moisture (spit to you and me) out of the expensive microphone components. These devices also do a good job of reducing plosives, such as popped Ps, Bs, and so forth. Get the kind that attaches to the mic stand and can be positioned easily between your mouth and the mic (http://www.popfilter.com). In a pinch, you can make a pop filter from a coat hanger and some (clean) pantyhose, but professionally-made ones are inexpensive and look a lot better! Avoid those foam filters that slip over the top of the microphone and look like oversized clown noses. These actually muffle the sound.

The Neumann TLM 103 is a popular microphone choice for recording voice.

Microphone Care

Handle your precious mic carefully. Don't blow into it, drop it, immerse it in water, play ring toss with it, or generally abuse it. Harlan feels strongly that you should never taunt your microphone or blame it for a lousy interpretation, but that's just his opinion. When it's not on its stand working for you, put the mic away in its case. Moisture and dust are anathemas. (Wow, we knew that Word-A-Day calendar would come in handy.) Keep the mic away from both of those evils. Jeffrey packs his mics away with those "Do Not Eat" silica packs. They absorb excess moisture easily—no fuss, no muss, and no snacking.

Microphone Preamps

Remember we said that microphones deliver electricity that can then be recorded. That's true, except the amount of electricity is too small. You need to boost or amplify a microphone's output before you can do anything else with it. For this, you need a microphone preamplifier whose purpose is to amplify the low-level microphone signal up to what is called *line-level*. This higher level can then feed mixers and computers. Preamps come in three flavors: mixers, stand-alone, and computer audio interfaces.

Do we hear you saying, "What about the dinky microphone input on the soundcard that came with my computer?" Guess what: That little hole accepts the plug from the garbage microphone you threw out earlier in this chapter. It's not a high-quality, low-noise microphone preamp suitable for serious voice recording. Surprise! We never recommend using it, so you won't use it either. In fact, let's just forget you mentioned it at all and quietly move on. Okay?

Mixer

As its name implies, a *mixer* lets you hook up many different sound sources and combine or mix them in new ways. Mixers come in all shapes and sizes (and dollar amounts!), and many include the proper input and pre-amp you need to work with your microphone. Quality microphones use those round tube-shaped three-prong XLR connectors, so make sure your mixer accepts that kind of plug. Because you will probably use only one microphone, most mixers have several extra inputs you'll never need. That's okay; the extra knobs and switches can really impress some people who need some impressing, and that alone is worth the price of admission.

One very important point: If you selected a condenser microphone, you must make sure the mixer you buy has *phantom power*. This spooky term merely means the mixer can supply the necessary power your condenser microphone needs to function properly. If the mixer you buy lacks this feature, your cool mic won't work. Dynamic microphones don't need power, so any mixer that accepts a microphone input will suffice. Also, some condensers work on batteries, but that is the exception more than the rule.

Many manufacturers make mixers with mic inputs, phantom power, and low-noise microphone preamps. You can't go wrong with models by Mackie and Behringer. The Mackie 1202VLZ Pro ($400; http://www.mackie.com) has enough inputs for four microphones, while the Behringer Eurorack

MX602 ($80; http://www.behringer.com) has two inputs. Both feature phantom power and low noise operation.

A small mixer, such as this one from Mackie, is ideal for voice recording.

Stand-Alone Microphone Preamp

Instead of a mixer, you can use a dedicated microphone preamp. They are built for one purpose—to provide a clean, low-noise preamp for high-quality microphones. Again, you need one that supplies phantom power for the same reasons mentioned earlier.

For straightforward microphone preamps, you can choose among the DBX Mini-Pre Tube Mic Pre-amp ($100; http://www.dbxpro.com), the ART Tube MP Studio V3 Mic Pre-amp ($120; http://www.artproaudio.com), and the PreSonus BlueTube Stereo Microphone Pre-amp ($150; http://www.presonus.com). You'll notice all three of these devices reference "tube" technology. That means they use a vacuum tube in the amplification stage instead of a solid state amplifier. So what? Many pros agree that tubes add pleasing warmth to the microphone's sound. Anything that helps present your voice in the best light can't be bad, right?

Other stand-alone preamps include the Focusrite Trak Master ($400; http://www.focusrite.com), DBX Pro Vocal ($300), and the Roland MMP-2 Mic Modeling Preamp ($600; http://www.roland.com). These are built more for music recording and have extra bells and whistles you don't really need and probably won't ever use. Harlan uses the preamp in his TL Audio Indigo compressor/EQ/preamp (http://www.tlaudio.co.uk). If only the best will work for you, consider the Avalon VT737SP ($2000; http://www. avalondesign.com)!

Audio Interface

Several computer audio interfaces available today include the preamp you need. These external sound devices accept balanced microphone inputs and even supply phantom power. They all include headphone outputs so you can monitor as you record your voice. Although some of the choices require installing a card inside your computer, others work through the USB or FireWire port on your computer; you simply plug it in and go.

We highly recommend you take the external audio interface approach when setting up your studio. These devices are a terrific choice because you not only get the preamp you need to work with your microphone, you also get a top-quality external ADC (at up to 24 bits, too!) that will make what you record sound far superior to what you'll get from the el-cheapo soundcard installed on your computer. Choices in this range include the Edirol UA-5 or UA-25 ($300 and $400; http://www.edirol.com), Sound Devices USB/Pre ($600; http://www.sounddevices.com), the M-Audio FW410 ($399; http://www.m-audio.com), or the Mackie Spike ($300; http://www.mackie.com).

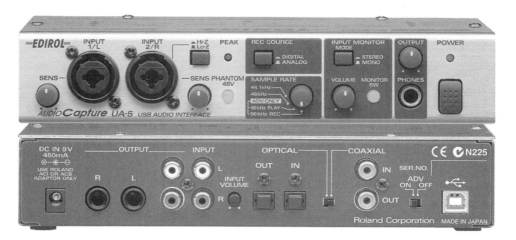

Audio interfaces offer mic preamps, headphone monitoring, and analog-to-digital converters in one compact box that plugs into the computer's USB or FireWire port.

Another big bonus of the plug-and-play method is that these interfaces can be used on multiple computers. Harlan uses his Mackie Spike on his home computer, on his wife's computer the day a virus brought his fiefdom to a crashing halt, and on his laptop when he's on the road. Jeffrey has several soundcards that also move from computer to computer depending on what he's doing and where.

Digital Recording Software

We've already discussed your need for a quality computer to serve as the center of your recording studio. The next critical component is the recording software. You want something that is easy to use, but powerful enough to help you do a good job.

For audio software, choose either a sound editor or a multitrack system. Sound editors essentially let you record and edit mono or stereo files. Multitracks let you combine several different recordings on separate, fully synchronized tracks. This gives you the greatest control over a project's different sound elements, such as music and sound effects. If you plan to do more extensive sound recording, such as producing finished radio spots, multitrack software would be mandatory.

Thankfully, a simple sound editor is all you need for most voice work. Any audio software capable of recording will suffice. The Sony Media Software Sound Forge Audio Studio software is a slightly stripped-down version of their very popular, full-featured, and professional Sound Forge 7 application (http://mediasoftware.sonypictures.com). You can easily record, edit, process, and deliver your finished voice tracks with this software. The cost? A mere $70. Audacity is a simple—and free—sound editor (http://audacity.sourceforge.net) that runs on Windows PCs and Macs. GoldWave is another inexpensive choice ($55; http://www.goldwave.com) for PCs.

Visit these Web sites to download and install trial versions. Play around with the software to see what works for you before getting out your plastic.

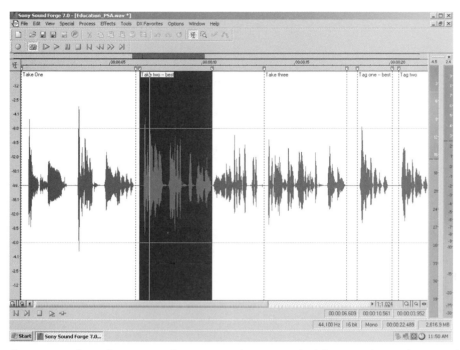

The Sony Media Software Sound Forge 7 application is ideal for recording, editing, and delivering voice tracks.

For multitrack software, Adobe makes Audition. With this software you can record, edit, combine, mix, and master up to 128 separate tracks. Sony Media Software weighs in with their Vegas 5 package which is a similarly powered audio engine attached to an even more powerful non-linear video editor. Harlan uses Audition, while Jeffrey uses the Vegas package (because he needs the video features in addition to the audio tools). And besides, if you haven't realized it already, Harlan and Jeffrey love being contrarians so they have something to argue about.

Other choices include Tracktion ($80; http://www.mackie.com), which prides itself on how easy it is to learn. This software is included free of charge with the Mackie Spike audio interface, too. Another nice tool is n-Track ($49, 24-bit version, $79; http://www.ntrack.com). There is even a free version of the ubiquitous Pro Tools (http://www.digidesign.com). Check out Sonic Spot (http://www.sonicspot.com) for links to demos, freeware, and shareware recording software and utilities.

Adobe Audition is another PC-based audio production tool.

For the Mac crowd, BIAS Peak (http://www.bias-inc.com) is the standard for mono and stereo recording and editing. It has a rich feature set that will serve you well for the majority of your audio tasks.

How to use these software products is the subject of Chapter 4, "Basic Production Procedures." Stay tuned.

Other Gear You Must Have

Enough already, right? You've already drained your savings by buying a microphone, stand, preamp, computer, audio interface, cables, and software. What else could you possibly need?

You need a way to listen to what you record. That means a pair of quality headphones and speakers are critical. You need to be sure what you record will sound the same when people play it back in their homes and offices. You can't risk letting cheap speakers lie about what's really on your recordings.

Headphones are useful, but they're not for making critical audio judgments. In other words, don't rely on headphones for the final recording. Most people listen on speakers, and what sounds good on headphones versus what sounds right on speakers can be completely different. Instead, wear headphones when you record so you can hear what's going on. Use them to check your finished recordings for background noises and other junk you might miss when listening on speakers. Don't let them have the final word, though. Always check your recordings on real speakers before you decide what sounds right.

Avoid open-ear-design headphones, such as those that come with portable CD players. Use closed-ear models that sit closer to your ears, surrounding them. They shut out outside sounds better and keep the sound in your headphones from feeding back through the microphone. Ouch, that can really hurt your ears (not to mention your equipment). There are a myriad of choices for less than $40. Slip on a pair and check for comfort and fit before buying. You might consider wireless headphones because they make it easier to roam around your studio unencumbered. However, sometimes wireless devices can pick up extraneous noises such as cab dispatchers or nearby radio stations.

If you want to sound like a hip professional (or a professional hippie), use the slang term "cans" when referring to headphones, as in, "Dude, I can't hear myself in the cans." This is not the same thing as "going to the can," the subject of our next book.

You also need a set of speakers to monitor your sound recordings and to make critical judgments about their quality. You know already, of course, that we're going to trash the little speakers that came with your computer. Frankly, they just won't cut it. You won't really be sure whether what you're hearing is an accurate reflection of what you're recording. These speakers are useful for one thing—to hear how your voice will sound on computer speakers. If your voice recording is destined for the Internet, checking on those computer speakers is perfect. Most people will hear your performance through them, so it makes sense to use them in this situation.

That said, you still need a better set of quality speakers for other voice work. Ready for more slang? Speakers are called *monitors* in the audio trade. And monitors don't come cheap. You have two choices: passive and active monitors. *Passive monitors* require a separate amplifier to power them. *Active monitors* include an amplifier in the speaker cabinet. Active monitors are often called *powered monitors*, and they are really the way to go. Remember that you can play your monitors in a hall, but they are not hall monitors!

Roland's MA8 Micro monitors ($100/pair; http://www.roland.com) look like typical computer speakers, but they are far more accurate. Alesis M1 Active Studio monitors ($500/pair; http://www.alesis.com); M-Audio BX5 ($300/pair; http://www.m-audio.com); Event's 20/20bas V2 ($900/pair); and Behringer B2031 Truth ($400/pair; http://www.behringer.com) are all excellent choices. Harlan is enamored with his Mackie HR624 ($600/pair; http://www.mackie.com), while Jeffrey loves his Event 20/20s (although he uses the M-Audio LX4 system for surround-sound work).

The next little extra doodad you might need is an analog phone patch or ISDN digital phone patch. These devices let you communicate with a producer or director by phone while recording in your studio. You hear their suggestions and they hear you as you record, similar to a long-distance intercom. We treat this subject in greater detail in Chapter 5, "Long-Distance Direction: All about Phone Patches and ISDN."

Another useful piece of gear is a music stand. It's perfect for holding your script while you read. If you use your hands when talking, then a stand is a must or you risk recording your script rattling about during your greatest performance ever.

Setting Up the Room

You need a space in which to record and a place for the computer and other recording gear. They can be one and the same or they can be separate rooms. Spare bedrooms and basements make good spaces, but even a corner of your living room can work. Don't try to record next to the computer because it will most likely be too noisy—you don't want that background noise ruining your voice tracks.

Get a decent desk designed to hold a computer. There should be enough room for the CPU, monitor, keyboard, mouse, and printer. Invest in a quality chair, too. You'll spend a lot of time working at the computer, so you deserve to be comfortable. The office superstores have plenty of furniture from which to choose. Jeffrey likes the selection at IKEA, too.

Your desk needs space to hold the monitor speakers you bought, too. If not, you'll need to invest in stands to support them. Proper speaker positioning is critical. You want the speakers at ear level with no obstructions in their way. Position them so that the two speakers and your head form the three points of an equilateral triangle.

Harlan uses a desk made specifically for audio gear by Omnirax Studio Furniture. Geez, he has a lot of stuff.

A single desk works for Jeffrey, with other audio gear located on a nearby rack.

With the basic office space ready, find a nearby area to record your voice. An echo-y space, such as a large room or tiled bathroom, just won't work. Even most bedrooms are too bright and bouncy, what engineers call "live sounding" for recording, which only means you'll hear more of the room itself than your voice. You know the sound—the hollow, mushy, and noisy quality of everybody's home videos. Voice work is better served by a tight, intimate quality, so find a suitable recording space.

There are two issues to keep in mind. One, you need to keep unwanted sounds from being picked up when you're recording. And two, you need a quiet, acoustically dead space that doesn't have its own sound. To keep sounds out of a room, you need to soundproof it. To make a room sound good, it needs acoustic treatment.

It's neither easy nor cheap to keep noise entirely out of a space, so don't even bother trying to soundproof a room. Instead, look for a space that's reasonably quiet already and set up your recording area in it. Sometimes recording at a different time of day can make the difference between quiet and noisy recordings. Take advantage of these opportunities. If you live near an airport or busy highway, find a different place to record rather than trying to fight the noise. You won't win.

Choose an interior space away from windows and outside doors, such as a large walk-in closet. If it's filled with clothing, it should sound just about perfect for recording voice. If it's fairly bare, the closet will sound boxy. Move some soft furnishings into it, such as pillows, sheets, blankets, towels, and more clothing. It's another excuse to go shopping: New wardrobe equals acoustic treatment for home studio. We are waiting for the tax court's ruling on this as a viable deduction, however, so consider that just a clever comment for now.

When a landscaping crew's noises made their way into one of Harlan's sessions, he knew he needed an acoustic solution. Though he lived in a quiet neighborhood, he couldn't take the chance of critical work being ruined. Rather than build a recording space, he opted for a ready-made portable sound enclosure designed specifically for voice work. These little 3.5' × 5' booths can both keep noise out and provide a dead space for recording. And since they set up and break down easily, Harlan was able to take the room with him when he moved. You can't do that with permanently-installed expensive soundproofing or acoustical treatment. Be prepared to pay for this luxury, though. A Whisper Room (http://www. whisperroom.com) can cost upwards of $3,000, as can similar products from VocalBooth (http://www.vocalbooth.com).

Ready-made, portable sound enclosures work well for serious voice recording.

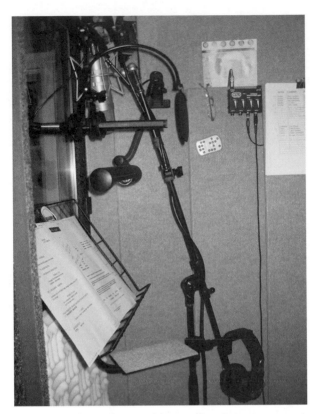

Another ready-made, portable sound enclosure

Building a Recording Booth

If the closet idea doesn't work and a ready-made sound booth is beyond your budget, consider building a little sound enclosure yourself. Set up a three-sided enclosure in a corner of a room by hanging three heavy, quilted moving blankets from the ceiling. Buy a few hooks and screw them into the ceiling. Buy some heavy picture-hanging wire, loop it over the hooks, punch the other end through the blankets, and tie it off. To keep the wire from ripping the blankets, install grommets. For best results, hang the curtain loosely. Double the enclosure with another set of blankets about six to eight inches outside and away from the first set to make the space even quieter. This basically forms a tent within another tent.

If your floor is hard, place a heavy throw rug underfoot. Also, stack some pillows in the corner where there are no blankets (though you could easily hang another blanket there if you want). Set up your mic inside this enclosure with your back to the corner, and then start recording. When you're finished, pull down the blankets, fold them up, and put them away.

Of course you'll have the hooks in the ceiling, but a little paint will help them blend in.

This idea creates a suitable recording space around the microphone for capturing the full tone of your voice. It won't keep loud noises from ruining a take, but it will remove the room sound from the recordings sufficiently.

Building a Different Recording Booth

Alternatively, you can build this standing portable booth using supplies you can buy at a local home center and from Markertek (http://www.markertek.com).

Buy three 36" bi-fold luan closet doors. These come unfinished in kits, complete with hinges. Buy one sheet of 54" × 54" × 2" Markerfoam Acoustic Foam and one sheet of 54" × 54" × 3" Markerfoam Acoustic Foam. Cut the foam pieces into six 18"-wide sections.

Buy one tube of Markerstik foam adhesive and use it to attach the foam to the inside of the closet door panels about four to six inches from the top. Put a two-inch piece on one panel and a three-inch piece on the other until you have foam on all six sections of the luan doors. Adjust where you place the foam depending on whether you'll stand or sit when recording. You want the foam to surround you, not the bare door panels. Buy more foam if you need to cover more of the door space.

Insert the hinge pins into the two-section doors and stand them up by bending the foam-covered doors in slightly. Set up a booth around your microphone using the three door sections. This booth reduces extraneous noise around the mic and creates a dry, quiet space in which to record your voice. Remove the hinge pins to break down the booth and store the sections when not in use. Better still, decorate the outside of the booth and use it as functional room divider. Chic!

Building a VO Box

Douglas Spotted Eagle, Grammy-winning artist, producer, sound designer, videomaker, writer, and respected authority on all things musical, sound, and video, designed and uses a simple, inexpensive, and portable VO box. It's perfect for reducing room noises around the mic while producing a fuller, more natural-sounding voice.

Even your dining room can sound good. Build a tabletop voice box using foam core and acoustic foam to keep out unwanted noise and provide a fuller sound when recording.

Buy a sheet 4' × 4' × 1/4" plywood or even sturdy foam core and cut it into four 24" × 24" sections. Also, buy four 24" × 24" pieces of acoustic foam. The two-inch foam is fine, but three-inch foam is better. You can use foam manufactured by SONEX (http://www.sonex.com), Auralex (http://www.auralex.com), or Markertek. Attach the foam to the cut plywood or foam core sections using an adhesive that is safe for foam, such as Scotch 76 spray adhesive or Markerstik foam adhesive.

On the table or desk you will record at, use the sections to build a three-sided box. If you're using foam core, tape the sections together with gaffers or duct tape. You can tape the plywood together or use hinges, if you're so inclined. Make sure you face the foam to the inside of the box. Next, lay the fourth section on top of the box you built. If you prefer to stand, use a higher table or bookshelf to hold your VO box.

With your mic mounted on a desk stand, put it inside the box about 10 inches from the front. Run the cord out under the box you built. Also, place a folded towel under the mic stand to reduce table noise from being picked up by the mic. Experiment with moving the microphone inside the box to get the sound you want.

Now deliver your performance into the mic inside the box as usual. The VO box will keep many unwanted sounds from ruining your recordings, and it also will make your voice sound great.

Don't Be Shy: Ask for Help

Consider asking an experienced local recording engineer for help selecting equipment and setting up your studio. You should offer to pay for this expertise either with money or some like trade. Perhaps the engineer needs a voice for a project, such as the studio's answering machine.

Well, there you have it. You now know just what you need to put together your own recording studio that is perfect for recording your voice. Time to go shopping!

4 } Basic Production Procedures

You have the gear you need; now it's time to hook it up and start recording your voice. The basic recording chain, or *signal path*, is mouth to microphone to preamp to soundcard (or other audio interface) to computer software, with the output of the software going back through the soundcard and on to speakers or headphones.

First, get your computer ready for recording. Hook up the CPU, mouse, keyboard, and such per the manufacturer's instructions. Install the software you selected and get it launched and ready onscreen. If you're using a stand-alone microphone preamp or mixer, connect its line output to the corresponding line input on your computer soundcard. If you use an external audio interface, connect it to the computer through its own cable (usually USB or FireWire).

External audio interfaces usually need special software, called *drivers*, to work correctly. You'll have to install them, too. Follow the instructions provided by the maker. Also, it's usually a good idea to check the company's Web site for the latest software drivers. Often the drivers included with the hardware are outdated. Don't forget to connect the audio interface's line output (which might say "headphone out") to your powered monitors or to your amplifier if you're using passive (non-amplified) speakers.

You'll have to refer to the instructions that came with your gear to make sure you've hooked it up correctly. Ask a knowledgeable friend or relative or hire a pro to get everything up and running if you're truly stumped.

Next, get your recording area ready. Assemble your sound booth, if you have one, and then your gear—the microphone, its stand, your music stand headphones, and a chair or stool if you prefer to sit while recording, although most VOs prefer to stand. If you do need a chair, for example when recording long-form narrations or recorded books, make sure it's quiet and free of squeaks. Noisy fabrics, such as leather and antique wooden chairs, will mar your recordings as they compete with your voice for attention. Imagine FDR's speech if it had been, "The only thing we have to fear is…SQUEAK…fear itself." Doesn't have the same impact, does it?

Your voice can also bounce off the music stand you use to hold your copy. That sound can bounce back into the microphone and adversely affect the quality of your recording. Drape a heavy cloth, fluffy bath towel, or carpet remnant over the stand to minimize this effect. Be careful of nearby hard surfaces, such as walls and windows; they too can reflect sound back to the microphone. Move away from them altogether or soften them through fabrics and acoustic treatments. Also, get closer to the microphone to separate your voice from any ill effects of the room. A good starting point is to leave about the width of your hand between the mic and your lips. It might seem close at first (you'll get used to it), but the sound will be much clearer, cleaner, and free from any room sound. When using the mic and setting levels, you want to maximize the signal-to-noise ratio. Basically, you want a loud, clean signal (your voice) and little or no noise (hum, hiss, background sounds, paper rustles, and so on). Getting close to the mic and using a directional mic helps. Properly setting the recording levels (discussed in a moment) to be as loud as possible without clipping is equally important. You want your performance to be louder in relation to everything else going on around you. This also reduces the effect of the room—you don't want your performance to sound as if you recorded it in a tunnel.

Put the microphone in its shock-mount and attach one end of the microphone cable to it. Wrap the mic cable loosely around the stand to the floor. This prevents accidentally catching the cable with your arm, clothing, or your foot. You don't want to trip and pull the microphone down with a crash. Condensers are fragile, so treat them nicely. Also, make sure the cable isn't bent or crimped and that there isn't too much pressure on the connector where it is attached to the mic.

Run the cable to your preamp. Use tape or a throw rug to hold down the wire so no one trips over it. Plug the other end of the mic cable into your preamp, mixer, or audio interface. It's a good idea to make sure any phantom power is switched off before plugging or unplugging microphone cables. The sudden jolt of electricity can ruin a condenser mic. It's also imperative at this point to keep all volume controls on your mixer, preamp, or interface off. If you don't, you risk sending a loud pop through your gear that can destroy a component or even blow a speaker. Get in the habit of turning your speakers and/or headphones down or off when unplugging cables and when turning on or off phantom power.

If your microphone is positioned too close to your speakers, you risk creating the high-pitched whine called *feedback* that preceded every announcement over the loudspeaker in high school, ruining the perfectly good nap you were enjoying in homeroom. Just turn the speakers off, and use your headphones in your recording area instead. Feedback occurs when the microphone sends sound to speakers and then picks up the same sound coming from the speakers and sends it back around again and again. Feedback is an oscillating sound loop that is hell on the ears and your recording gear. Need we say it again? Open mic? Turn the monitors off!

With the volume down (see how we can't help bringing this up over and over?) on both the mic preamp and the speakers, make sure all the connections are secure, and then engage the phantom power switch if you're using a condenser microphone. (Leave it off if you're using a dynamic mic.) Although the microphone should begin working immediately, most people agree that letting it warm up a bit results in a better sound. Five minutes is sufficient—longer if you're using a tube microphone, tube preamp, or both. And it couldn't hurt to turn off the phantom power when you are finished recording.

Setting Levels outside the Box

Now comes the tricky part. How do you set a level for the microphone and your headphones when you have to be in two places at once—at the mic and at the computer? (Harlan had his arms surgically lengthened, which explains why his hands drag on the ground when he walks.) You can accomplish this by simply making some tests. You can, of course, move the microphone temporarily out of your sound booth and get some basic levels while near the computer. But then it's best to return it to the booth and refine the levels once again.

It'll save time if you can press a relative or friend for help with this step. Better still, hire a professional sound engineer to hook up your gear correctly and help you set basic levels. A few dollars spent here can make your life so much easier later.

Thankfully, once you determine the optimum recording level for your voice, it's pretty much set it and forget it. Once you have those levels picked, use a china marker, pieces of tape, or sticky notes to mark the settings. Also, write down your settings, just in case you forget or some innocent person diddles with your knobs unexpectedly. Store this piece of paper where you can find it in a pinch. Both Jeffrey and Harlan have kids, and you can imagine how tempting it is for a child to turn all those shiny knobs and slide those faders up and down while Dad's out of the studio. Take it from us—write those settings down!

How to Work a Mic

Before you begin speaking, turn slightly away from the mic, take a breath, exhale, and then take another breath. Now open your mouth, turn toward the mic, and start speaking. This reduces the risk of recording sharp intakes of breath and lip smacks at sentence starts. Of course you can edit them out, but why waste precious time when you can do it right in the first place?

Pull your head back or even rock back slightly on your heels, thereby moving about four to eight inches away from the mic during loud passages. If you double the distance between your mouth and the mic, you'll cut the volume in half. Be aware that you'll pick up more room and less voice the farther you speak from the mic.

Bring your index finger up to your lips on bad plosive "p" words to reduce pops.

Also, remove jangling jewelry (earrings, bracelets, and such) before recording. Avoid polyester or over-starched clothes that rustle, too. And please, don't turn away from the mic or put your hands (or other objects) in front of your mouth while you speak. These bad habits interfere with getting a quality recording.

The best way to avoid the dreaded dry mouth and the affiliated clicks and pops heard in the recording is to prevent them in the first place. Never drink milk or eat salty foods before recording. Harlan has found through embarrassing experience that it's best to eschew (Wow, do we have a vocabulary or what?) Chinese food before a session due to its high salt content and the resulting mouth noise. Keep some tepid water handy. (Water that is too cold freezes the vocal cords.) Take a plastic bag with a few apple slices into the booth, too. That can really help get the juices flowing and the clicks removed before they start.

And there's a secret called "Entertainer's Secret Throat Relief" that helps with dry mouth, hoarseness, and raspy throat. Come to think of it, it's not a secret now, is it? Anyway, this handy little spray bottle contains some magical ingredients, such as aloe vera, that really help, particularly if you are doing long sessions. It's available online at http://www.entertainers-secret.com, by phone at 800-308-7452, or from our friends at Everything VO http://www.everythingvo.com. There you'll find a lot of other unique VO things as well, such as Marsha Mason's Killer Throat Spray, *The Voice Over Resource Guide*, and those spiffy "As Heard on TV" VO baseball caps created by some VO guy named Harlan something.

If you use a stand-alone preamp or other audio interface, there's probably a single knob for setting the level. Always start with the level completely down and off and then slowly increase it while speaking. Some devices include a meter that helps you set the optimum level. You'll see a row of little lights, called LEDs, with number markings: −20, −10, −5, −3, 0. The zero is the important one.

If the meters are analog, you want the level of your voice to peak at or just below zero. That means the majority of your speaking should stay well below the 0 and only occasionally, such as on a particularly loud word or phrase, light it up. If you're seeing the −5 and −3 continuously lit, you're doing fine.

If the peak meter is for a digital device, such as an external audio interface, your speaking should stay well below the 0 and *never* light it up. In the digital world, unlike the analog world, once you go over zero you pretty much record zero. All those little ones and zeros become garbage to the computer, and it, to put it not so politely, pukes on you. Refer to your gear's owner's manual to see what your meters are telling you. If you use a mixer as your preamp, there are usually extra controls. First, there may be a switch labeled Mic–Line. Switch this to Mic to tell the mixer you've plugged in a microphone. Along the lower edge of the mixer, there will be a channel knob or sliding fader with adjacent negative number markings leading up to zero. Set this at zero to start.

Now look for another knob, usually along the upper part of the mixer near that Mic–Line switch. It might be called Input Trim, Gain, or something similar. This controls the mixer's preamp volume. Start with this knob fully counterclockwise and slowly increase the preamp volume while speaking. Use the mixer's meters to set the optimum level as described earlier.

The process for setting a level going from the preamp to the computer can vary greatly. A mixer might have an output or master level adjustment. If so, set it to zero and make level adjustments with the mic preamp volume or input trim. A stand-alone mic preamp and/or external audio interface may also have an output knob. Set it to its optimum position. Use the input volume control to set a good recording level.

The Sens knob (input level) on the Edirol UA-5 controls the mic gain. However, its output knob only controls the volume going to the speakers or headphones. There is no separate output level adjustment going to the computer.

Congratulations. You've hooked up the mic, powered it up, and set the correct recording level at the input stage of your recording. If the output of your preamp is connected properly, you can now check the level going to the computer.

Setting Levels inside the Box

Make sure you hook up the output of your mixer or separate preamp into your soundcard. Typically, that's going to be the Line In connection. If you use a USB- or FireWire-based recording interface, the corresponding cable carries your signal down the line to the computer. These devices do their digitizing outside of the computer and only send the little digital zeros and ones to the computer.

Understand this *really* important point. The audio interface or sound-card software controls the level of the audio you record. There are no level adjustments in the audio recording software. While you can monitor the levels with the software, the actual adjustments—louder or softer—must be made at the mixer/preamp/audio interface that you use.

However, depending on the hardware you use, you may have to make additional level settings using special software, called a *driver*, installed on the computer. This driver software typically "talks" to the soundcard and sits between the hardware outside the computer and the recording software you use. If this applies to your situation, set the input source—what the soundcard records and the level. Select Line In and set the volume control between 75 and 100 percent. Adjust the volume going to the audio inter-face using the mixer or preamp stage instead. If you know you've set the level there correctly, fiddle with this software control knob until the levels match. Better still, use a test tone to match levels. (See the sidebar entitled "VU for Vous?") Also, refer to the manuals that came with your computer and/or audio gear for suggestions.

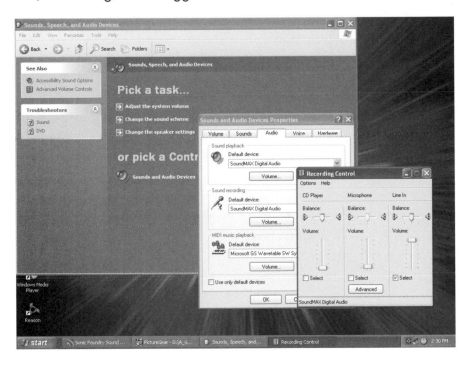

Windows XP includes software that controls what the internal soundcard records, as well as the associated input volume level. Notice the Line In input source is selected and the volume is at 100 percent.

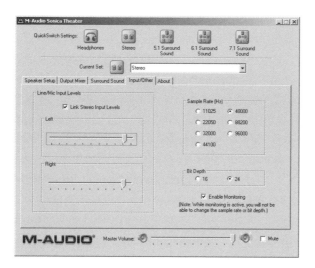

The M-Audio Sonica Theater is an external USB-based soundcard that uses a special software program for controlling both input and output levels. This device only accepts Line In (it has no mic preamps), but it has six outputs Jeffrey uses for 5.1 surround-sound projects.

With your levels matched, it's time to start recording. Your software might differ somewhat from the examples used here. These differences are usually subtle and often cosmetic in nature. Understanding basic recording concepts is far more important than learning a specific application. If you can set levels and get a decent sound down, it really doesn't matter which software you use. The similarities are close enough that you will begin to feel comfortable with any basic recording software package.

For this example (and throughout the book), we'll use the Sony Media Software Sound Forge 7 package. Of course we are assuming you have a basic understanding of working with software on a computer, including how to navigate, open, and save a file, and so forth.

The Sound Forge application has a set of transport controls that should look familiar. If you've ever used any kind of recorder, you've seen similar buttons. To start recording, simply click the big, red Record button. A dialog box will pop up, offering a bevy of functions, which is pretty much the same thing as a plethora of options—take your choice. First, set your recording attributes. It's best to record your voice at the highest sampling rate and bit depth your computer hardware can handle. Be aware that the limitations of your soundcard/audio interface (and even your recording software) will dictate the sampling rate and bit depth you can actually use. Because CD quality is 44,100 Hz and 16 bits, this should be the *minimum* setting at which you record. The last time we checked, most humans had only one mouth, so you are a monophonic instrument. There's no need to record your voice in stereo. Choose mono!

If 44,100 Hz and 16 bits is the *minimum* setting, what is the optimum sampling rate and bit depth? We both feel moving up to 48,000 Hz and 24 bits is ideal for serious recording, editing, and processing. The sound is more natural and open. You can always save the final version to a more suitable format, such as a CD-compatible file (44,100 Hz and 16 bits). And although you will probably "dumb down" your recorded files to the highly compressed MP3 format (for e-mailing), it is still better to start with the highest quality first. Ever hear your computer-savvy friends talk about GIGO? It's geek-speak for garbage in, garbage out!

Notice that the Record dialog box also includes a pair of recording level meters. If they are not active, click to select the Monitor check box. If you start talking into your microphone, you should see these meters jump around in response to your voice. These level meters show what the computer will record. Notice there is no level adjustment in the Sound Forge application. You need to set levels at your outboard equipment and/ or within the software that controls your audio interface (if that applies). Hopefully, you followed the previous advice and fixed the soundcard level between 75 and 100 percent, so reducing or increasing the level will take place at your preamp/mixer/audio interface as needed. The most efficient workflow is adjusting and tweaking levels in only one location with an eye on the software meters.

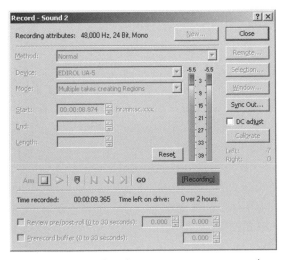

The Record dialog box lets you set up your recording's attributes and monitor the level.

We know this might sound confusing, but once you get it down, it's pretty much set and forget. Just remember that you need to check the microphone, its preamp (input and output), and the software that controls the audio interface. Adjustments to any and all of these settings affect the level of the sound you record.

Let's do a test recording. With the levels set, hit the red Record button in the dialog box and begin to speak. Try to avoid for the sake of tradition saying, "Mary had a little lamb." Try something like, "Wow, I'm actually recording my own voice professionally, right here at home, thanks to Jeffrey Fisher and Harlan Hogan. Maybe I should send them each a couple hundred bucks in gratitude." Record for about 15 seconds and then hit the Stop button. Close the dialog box and you'll see a file on your screen that looks something like this:

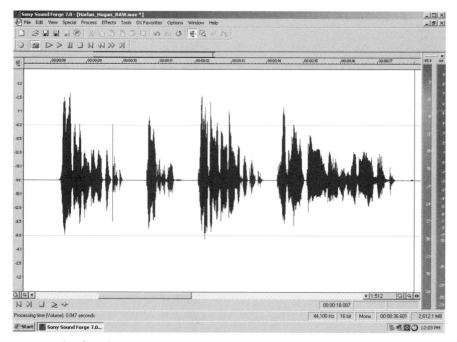

An example of Harlan's voice recorded on computer. Can you guess what he's saying?

You're looking at a two-dimensional representation of sound digitized by the computer. Neat, huh? Okay, maybe not that neat, but interesting in a visualize-a-waterbed kind of way. Play back the recording, watch, and listen. Do you see how the screen waveform changes depending on the words? Later, you'll be editing these little waveforms just like you would words in a word processing program.

Make sure you save and name your recording at this point. Windows XP saves digital audio as .wav files; Macs save it as .aiff files. Both formats are uncompressed, full-quality digital files. They are also somewhat large. A single minute of stereo CD-quality sound takes up 10 MB on the hard drive; a minute of mono takes half that—another good reason to record your voice in mono. Naturally files this large won't fit on floppy disks and are unwieldy to e-mail. Thankfully, there are file compression schemes that significantly reduce the size of these digital wave files, the most common being MP3. Chapter 7, "Untangling the World Wide Web" includes more on this subject.

Spying Good Levels Onscreen

A good recording level should look like the basic digital waveform shown previously. The overall level will be consistent, with a few peaks that don't exceed −6. If you set the level too low, it might look like this:

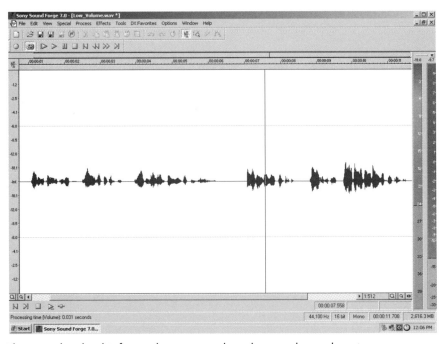

This recording level is far too low; turn up the volume and record again.

The level is too high if your recording looks like this:

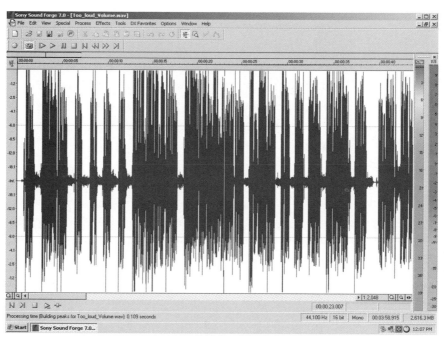

Whoa there! This level is way too high and will sound distorted.

Notice that the really loud parts are squared off or clipped at the top. They show up better when you zoom in; they look something like the picture below. This kind of distortion sounds like sandpaper rubbing on your ear. Yuck.

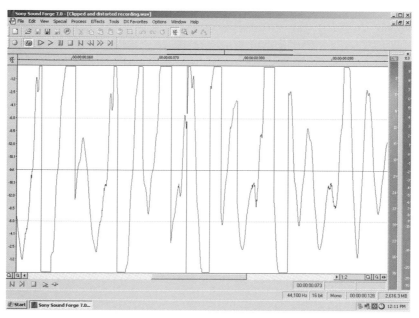

Zoom in to get a better view.

Your audio software should have controls for zooming in and out. Look for a little magnifying glass. It's often easier to work on your sound files when you zoom in a little. You can really see what you're doing so you can make better edits. Unfortunately, you may occasionally zoom in too far and get lost in zoom hell. If that happens, zoom out to regain your perspective. You might want to invest a few extra dollars in a mouse with a scrollwheel so you can seamlessly zoom in and out of the waveform; it will save you tons of time you'd otherwise waste constantly clicking on those magnifying glasses.

It's very important that you *never*, *ever* exceed 0 dB with a digital recording. Keep your loudest peaks below that, with the overall level even lower. Try peaking at between −6 and −10 dB below digital 0. Digital is a low-noise recording medium, so you can keep your levels much lower than you would in the old analog world of noisy recording tape. You might record a little hotter, depending on your voice and recording skills, but don't hit or exceed zero. Promise? If you do exceed digital zero, we suggest recording another take because the clipping distortion sounds terrible (and flags you as a flagrant amateur).

Make some additional recordings, adjusting the controls until you get consistent levels. You can always use mic technique, moving closer or farther away, to deal with particular situations. And since recording at home is low risk, you can always re-record a bit that didn't turn out quite right. Once you've made a few recordings, you'll get the hang of it. We have the utmost confidence in you! Really.

VU for Vous?

In the analog world, measuring the volume or level of an audio signal, whether coming from a microphone, guitar, or other sound source, required a volume unit or VU meter. A good level kept the meter between −3 and 0 dB, and it was okay to jump past the 0 occasionally. There was space, called *headroom*, to handle a quick peak without distorting.

In the digital world there is also a 0 dB maximum, but unlike its analog counterpart, it is not acceptable to exceed it. When you do, the resulting sound is distorted. It looks as if the sound waveform was clipped off with scissors, and it sounds strident, muffled, and nasty.

It's important to note that 0 dB analog is the equivalent to −20 dB on a digital meter. Run a steady tone through an analog mixer and set the levels so the meter stays at 0 dB. Connect this output to the computer and then set levels so that the steady tone reads −20 dB on the digital meter. This is the only way to make sure you've matched the output of your analog gear to the digital domain.

You can download the test tone from this book's Web site: http://www.audiosmartactors.com.

Getting Serious with the Microphone

With gear hooked up and basic levels adjusted, it's time to fine tune a few more things. Placing the microphone is the next critical adjustment. Minor changes can greatly affect the resulting sound. Don't be afraid to experiment a little, though these basic ideas should suffice for almost all the work you do. Also, make sure you do some additional level tests after moving the mic around.

Hang the mic from above on the end of a boom. Put it in the shock mount if you have one. Position the mic capsule (the part where the wire mesh is) so it is centered and even with the front of your mouth. Don't use the center of the mic housing itself as your reference. Make sure you center the business end of the mic—where the diaphragm resides—as your guide. You can usually see it through the grill that covers and protects it.

We mentioned before that you should keep the noise of the room and its particular sound signature out of your recordings. The easiest way to do so is to get close to the mic, about four to six inches away. If you use a shotgun, try six to ten inches as a starting point instead.

If you're a particularly quiet speaker or you're trying for that breathy, sensual female sound, get a little closer. Remember, there is a boost of the low-frequency bass content to your voice as you get closer to a cardioid mic. This can add fullness to thin voices, but it can make deep voices overly boomy. Let your ears judge what's best for your particular voice. Do some test recordings, play them back, and evaluate what you hear.

If you're a strong speaker back off a little, but not too much. You don't want your voice swimming around the room, making the recording sound like it was done in a bathroom or parking garage. Stay close and keep the room sound out of your recording. Adjust the recording levels instead to accommodate your loud mouth, which is a rather nice metaphor, if we do say ourselves. You'll sound drier, closer, and more intimate. "In your face," as we say in the trade—but we must hasten to add, not necessarily any smarter.

Be aware that the closer you are to the mic, the more mouth noises you'll pick up in your recording. Lips smacks, tongue action, and other gross-out noises have no place in polished performances. A little technique here can go a long way toward reducing unwanted sounds. Alternatively, you'll have to edit them out later. But that is the beauty of digital recording: Removing vocal mistakes is fast and easy.

Get close to the mic, and you run a much greater risk of popping Ps or Bs and introducing other loud peaks that can ruin good performances. To stop these plosives, position a nylon pop filter halfway between your lips and the mic. Next, raise the mic slightly so the bottom of the capsule is even with your upper lip. If that still doesn't work, try taping a pencil across the outside of the mic, centered over the capsule. The pencil keeps the puff of air from a P, B, or T from striking the diaphragm.

Another technique is to come in from the side instead of directly in front of the mic. Position the mic so it's between 20 and 30 degrees to the left or right of your mouth. Be sure to aim the mic capsule at your lips, though. This strategy keeps the mic out of your direct field of vision, making it easier to see the script. Best of all, side miking reduces plosives and some sibilance.

Example of proper miking

Example of alternative side miking

Sibilance has nothing to do with brothers and sisters. Sibilance refers to excessive "S" sounds in a recording. Record "Susie sells seashells by the seashore" and hit those Ss hard to hear what we mean. Even with a good recording level, they sound kind of distorted. Females tend to have a more sibilant quality to their voices. To fix this in your recordings, really work on positioning the mic—try side miking—until you find the best sound. It may take some fine adjustments to reach the goal. Of course, perfecting and practicing a cleaner, clearer delivery can really cut down on those S sounds, too.

You can reduce sibilance by applying some frequency-dependent compression and/or EQ after recording, but we'll get to that in Chapter 8, "Advanced Techniques." Until then, use this phrase to impress your friends: "Yeah, the sibilance was destroying the vibe, so I ran the DC offset, applied some frequency-dependent compression, EQed out the lows, normalized the output, and rendered an MP3." They won't know what the hell you're talking about. Then again, you might not know what the hell you're talking about either, but you will soon. For now, we'll take our cue from Billy S. again. "Have more than thou showest; speak less than thou knowest."

Keep on Tracking

Enough preparation already, right? Time to get down to business and do some serious recording. You've set up the gear, placed the microphone where it makes you sound your best, and checked and double-checked your levels. Let's go....

Basic recording is called *tracking* in the trade. It's where you record your various takes of the script. Each take is a separate performance or part of a performance. What are the characteristics of a good spoken-work recording? Clarity rules the day with a natural, pleasant quality to the voice a close second. We need to hear what you say clearly and in a way that makes us feel good without sounding phony or over-enunciated—a delicate balancing act. Also, you need to keep your recordings free of annoying mouth or other distracting noises, as well as distortion.

As an actor, you don't want the technology interfering with your ability to deliver lines satisfactorily. That's why we suggested all this preparation work up front. You can't be a computer or recording technician and a good performer at the same time. If you've taken the time to get all this basic stuff down before recording, you can simply turn everything on, press Record, step up to the mic, and perform your butt off.

Focus on the work and let the technical details of recording take care of themselves. Hopefully, you'll relax and can reach the state that Stanislavski described. "When an actor is completely absorbed by some profoundly moving objective so that he throws his whole being passionately into its execution, he reaches a state we call inspiration."

Record the sample scripts included here or choose something of your own that takes about a minute. A brief soliloquy is a good first project. Grab a copy of *Smithsonian* or *National Geographic* to read aloud. Start your software and get into record mode. Run through and record the piece a couple of times and then listen back. If you need to redo a few lines, do that now. Don't feel the need to necessarily complete your performance in one complete take. The beauty of digital recording is how easily you can edit bits and pieces from several takes into one seamless and polished performance.

SAMPLE SCRIPT:
"SHELL PRESENTS THE HAUNTINGS AT NAVY PIER"

Where's the *number one* place to have fun this Halloween season?

SFX: KIDS LAUGHING

Chicago's *number one* year round attraction—Navy Pier!

As Shell presents: The Hauntings…

SFX: PSYCHO-LIKE STRINGS UNDER

…at Navy Pier, now through Halloween.

From the free hayrides every day on Dock Street…

SFX: KIDS LAUGHING, CREAKING WHEELS

To Navy Pier's acclaimed Haunted House, this will be a Halloween to remember…

With live entertainment…

A kids' craft corner…

Trick-or-treating every Saturday…

SFX: "TRICK-OR-TREAT"

A costume contest every Sunday…

…and just for the little ones—Scarecrow Holler!

SFX: YOUNG KIDS, GIGGLING

Young or old, Navy Pier is the place to be this fall as Shell presents: The Hauntings at Navy Pier.

For more information, log on to www.navypier.com or call 312-595-PIER, and remember, Navy Pier is not just fun…it's haunting!

SFX: PSYCHO-LIKE STRINGS

SAMPLE SCRIPT:
"BEN"

SFX: BANK INTERIOR

Woman: (older)   Ben, everybody I know is refinancing their homes…

Ben: (older)   Neither a borrower nor a lender…

Woman: Don't start with the slogans…

Ben: A fool and his money…

Woman:	Is what we'll be, if we don't call Home Mortgage Center and refinance…
Ben:	Well, a penny saved is a penny…
Woman:	We are not talking pennies Ben; we're talking big bucks…
Ben:	And, the buck stops…
Woman:	Here. I'm calling right now.
SFX:	PHONE DIAL UNDER
Announcer:	At Home Mortgage Center all we do is home loans. If you're ready to buy a new house, refinance, or consolidate your bills with a home equity loan, call 1-800-555-1235 or visit us on the Web at hmc.com. We're the specialists in residential loans, at 1-800-555-1235. Home Mortgage Center—where all our calls are house calls.
SFX:	PHONE BEING HUNG UP
Woman:	Ben, HMC was great…. We can save on our mortgage payments and get a tax-deductible home-equity loan.
Ben:	The only thing certain is death and taxes…
Woman:	True. We'll save on our taxes, and I'm going to kill you if you utter one more "catchy phrase."
Ben:	Would "silence is golden" count?
Woman:	I'll let that one go…
Announcer:	HMC is an Illinois, Indiana, Wisconsin, and Michigan residential mortgage licensee.

When you're satisfied with your performances, save your files. Let's say that again because even with this caveat, you won't be human if you don't at some point forget to save the file you've just recorded. Usually you'll only make this mistake once, but it will inevitably be on something that was just perfect—if only you'd saved it. Create a folder for the project on your hard drive and keep all the files related to the project in the folder. This could include scripts, notes, and all your audio files. For larger projects, create subfolders in the main folder. For example, Jeffrey creates separate folders for voice, sound effects, music, and final mixes on his projects. Avoid cryptic files names; name your files in meaningful ways. For separate takes or versioning, consider using a number extension. Use the 001, 002, and so on format to keep the files in proper numerical order.

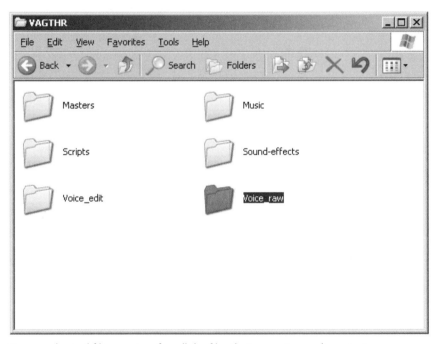

Create a logical filing system for all the files that comprise each project.

Before you move on to the editing stage, burn a quick backup CD (see the following sidebar, "Oh, My Aching Backup") and take a break. You need to rest your mind and ears and make the mental switch from performer to technician.

Oh, My Aching Backup

It's good practice to back up your work after a fruitful tracking session. Don't risk losing the best performance of your life due to some error on your part or the machinations of a malicious computer. After reviewing your takes to make sure there's enough raw material there, burn a quick data CD of the files you just recorded. This way you can always return to these original files no matter what happens later. We speak from experience; you won't ever regret making an extra backup. Blank CDs are cheap, and the time it takes to make a backup is far less than the time it would take to do an extensive piece all over again. Another option is to move copies of the original files to a different hard drive. This drive could be inside the computer or it could be an external drive connected via USB or FireWire. Jeffrey recommends the small flash "thumb" drives for quick backups and portability. The cheap 128-MB ones can hold about 25 minutes of mono voice recordings at full CD quality.

Make a point of backing up the final versions, too, on a different data CD or drive. Store these master CDs somewhere safe, away from your computer. For critical masters, make another copy and save it offsite with a friend or relative, or even in a safe deposit box.

How you make a backup depends on the software you have and whether you selected a computer with a CD writer. We address these issues in the Chapter 8 "Advanced Techniques."

Get Set to Edit

Listen to your raw tracks first on headphones. You need to do two things simultaneously. One, judge your performance and choose the best parts. Two, listen for recording baddies such as distortion, background sounds, and other glitches. These no-nos can come between takes—even phrases— and you don't want your roomie's toilet flush underscoring your best *Hamlet* "To be or not to be." Make notes on the script as you assess the recordings.

Use headphones at this point for another reason. If you record and edit in the same room, even with a makeshift booth, there may be noise on the recording that you'll miss on speakers. Your brain is rather adept at tuning out the general racket of your room (cars whizzing by outside, computer fan, heater kicking in and out, TV down the hall, and so on). You can easily ignore (as in not hear) the noise around you. Microphones aren't so smart; they hear *everything*. The noise of your surroundings may be part of your recording, too, but you won't hear it on speakers because of the noise in your room. The background noises are in *both* the recording and in the room itself.

A few years back Harlan was booked by a video production house to record a lengthy narration for Komatsu earth-moving equipment. When he arrived he was surprised to see they didn't have an audio booth, just a microphone on a stand smack-dab in the middle of the editing suite. All the whirling video drive noises, hard drive fans, and the clients fidgeting in their seats were dutifully recorded. In his headphones he could hear that the whole recording was going to be unusable, but he hesitated to say anything and figured the moment they listened to a playback, the obvious mistake would be heard and corrected. But when the track was played back—in the same noisy room—it sounded just fine! Not surprisingly, he was re-booked the following day at a proper recording studio to re-record the whole script once the client heard the tracks outside the video suite! So, headphones help at this stage by isolating your recording, warts and all.

If the sound checks out on headphones, switch to speakers for further evaluation and to make your editing choices. Before you do another thing, make a copy of the file you are going to edit. In the Sound Forge software, simply choose File > Save As and rename the file. If you named your original file Voice_001.wav, name the copy Copy_voice_001.wav. Work on the copy from now on. Leave the original as a backup in case you really make a mistake. Plus, if you burned a backup data CD as we suggested earlier, you have yet another safety net.

We hear you. Yes we actually can hear you. You're saying, "Geez, are these guys paranoid or what? Save, save, save, back up, back up, back up." You can call us paranoid—and if you do, we'll hear *that*, too. However, we call it experience. And experience has taught both of us— sometimes bitterly—that mistakes get made. So don't risk losing valuable, irreplaceable work—save it and back it up.

When you are working on the copy of your file, run a special utility called DC Offset. Sometimes a soundcard adds direct current (DC) to the audio being recorded. This might result in the waveform not being positioned correctly around the center line. The DC Offset utility automatically corrects this problem if it occurs. If you don't run this, you might hear clicks, pops, or other unwanted noises after editing or applying effects to your recording. As a rule, run the utility on every file you record before you start editing. Save it again. Then start to edit.

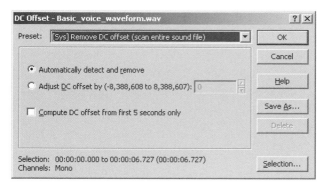

The Sound Forge application can automatically remove any DC offset from your files.

Use the notes you took when listening back to your raw tracks and begin to assemble a complete recording. You have two choices for working in an audio recording and editing program. One, you can edit the file directly. If you recorded everything in one file—several takes and line fixes—it's easier to simply edit out the mistakes and compile the best bits within that single file. Or, you can edit in a blank file. If you recorded in several different files, it's best to start with a blank file and copy and paste the best parts from those raw files into a complete version.

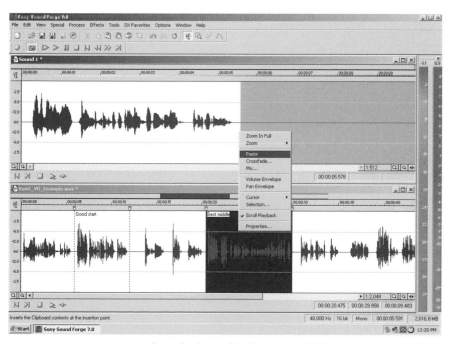

Sometimes it is easier to combine the best takes from several files into one main file.

In either case, get rid of all the unwanted parts and put the best performances in place first. There are probably some background noises from before you started in earnest, in between takes and so forth. Dump 'em.

Listen for lips smacks and other mouth noises and cut them out. In general, get the piece cleaned up and fixed into a (mostly) complete performance.

You can listen to the before and after versions of a voice track on http://www.audiosmartactors.com. The before has all the junk in it, while the after just keeps the main part.

Every Breath You Take

There is great division in the sound world about breathing. Specifically, some people cut out breaths and others leave them in. If you cut out every breath in a recording, your delivery will sound unnatural (unless that's what you're trying to achieve). If you leave the breaths in, they sometimes start to annoy listeners. Part of this is the unfortunate side effect of close miking your mouth. The mic hears every breath up close and accentuates it somewhat. In normal conversation, other people don't typically hear you breathe (the exception being in the closeness shared between two consenting adults), but recorded voice can sound unnaturally breathy.

Our advice? Work on your breathing—so you're not gasping for breath. *Catch breaths*—those quick inhales you take between long phrases—almost always sound horrible. Mark up the script by indicating natural breathing points to avoid these gasps for air, too. When you really feel the need for a large inhale, turn away from the mic slightly, take the big breath, turn back, and start speaking.

During editing you can cut out the breaths that add nothing to your performance, along with most catch breaths. You can tighten your performance by dumping these breaths and moving the adjacent words in their place. However, do leave the more natural-sounding breaths in place, even if they sound particularly pronounced. You can always reduce their volume level a little when editing.

Editing on Your Computer

Editing audio is really no different than editing a word processing document. You can even "see" the words, although they're not in any alphabet you'd recognize. Instead you see a two-dimensional waveform representation of the sound you recorded. Best of all, you can actually hear the words, too.

You just need to use your basic computer commands of select, delete, cut, copy, and paste. You select parts of the digital waveform by holding down the left mouse button and dragging it along the waveform. Then you can delete, cut, or copy the selection. It's easy to get rid of unwanted sections, and even rearrange them. Continue to trim the recording as needed.

When editing a sound file, you just need to remember to make edits where the waveform crosses the center line. Think of the center line as the space between words in a word processor. You wouldn't cut hal…fway in the middle of a word, would you? As you make selections in the audio editing software, make sure that both ends are at points where the waveform crosses the center line. Zoom in to be sure and adjust as needed. If you use the Sound Forge software, the keyboard shortcut Z makes sure your selection is proper.

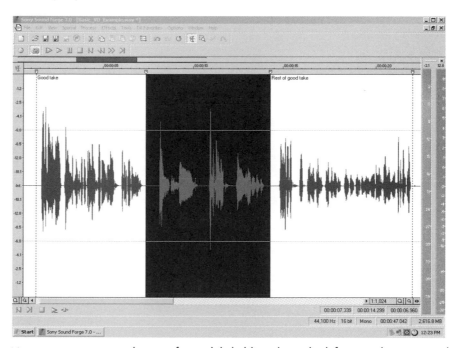

Move your mouse over the waveform while holding down the left mouse button to make a selection.

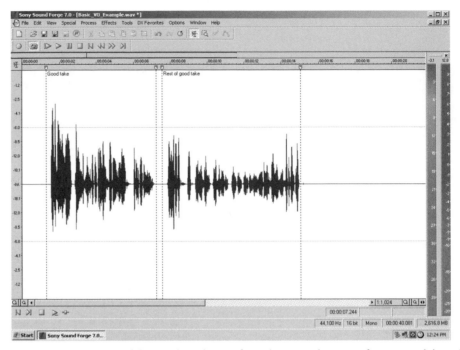

Notice how cutting (or deleting) the selection from the preceding waveform moved the adjacent sections closer together.

If you need to move a section from one place within the file to another (or from one file window to another), make the selection and cut it. This places the data in a temporary computer memory area called the *clipboard*. Next, position the cursor where you want to put the cut section by clicking your mouse. Paste the cut section in place. Take some time to work on your file until you're satisfied with how it sounds. When you've finished, save it.

If there are other problems with your voice recording, check out Chapter 8 for tips on how to fix the most common mistakes.

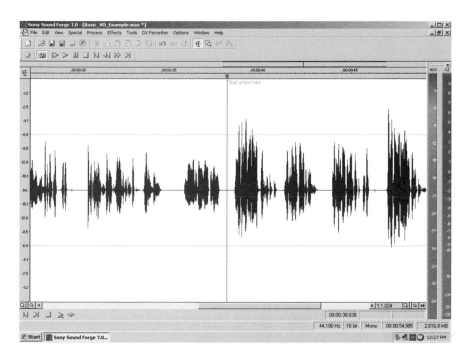

You can also insert markers in your file to make keeping track of sections, takes, flubs, and so forth easier.

Hooray! You've recorded, edited, saved, and finished your first voiceover performance. You deserve a standing ovation, roses, and great reviews. Or at least a stiff drink.

5 } Long-Distance Direction: All about Phone Patches and ISDN

So, you've got your home studio set up—well, almost all set up. Your recording studio, like your voice demo, is never, ever totally all done. So, you've got your home studio *almost* all set up and you have been sending MP3 auditions around the world, across the county, or just downtown. Inevitably, someone somewhere is going to ask you or your agent, "Can I direct the audition?"

Better yet, perhaps by now you are confident enough in your recording setup and experience to be doing honest-to-goodness going-on-the-air-tomorrow sessions from home. In that case, it's almost guaranteed that the producer will want to direct you. You'll need some way to take direction and record your voice while the agent, director, or producer hears what you are recording and helps you shape your reading. You'll need a "patch," which is another way of saying a long-distance intercom or talk-back system.

Phone Patches

The most common way of directing talent from a remote location is via a phone patch, and, as the name implies, it uses a plain old telephone line. We proudly avoided using the catchy techno-geek term for this, the POTS line, because, as much we love most jargon, POTS just sounds silly. The person directing the talent listens on a regular telephone line to your reading and gives you direction. Often the director will be in a distant recording studio, hearing you over a professional phone interface and studio speakers, but other times he or she will simply sit at a desk and listen on a regular or speaker phone. It's simple, basic, inexpensive, and it works well. There are a few tricky parts, though, and some additional equipment you'll need to make this work smoothly.

While you can spend a few bucks on a phone patch device that sits between your mixer and telephone, you can really go low-tech on this one. In an emergency or if you are really pressed for cash, you can simply record while holding the telephone up near your mouth. (We aren't recommending this, except *maybe* for an audition.) The producer will hear your reading but not the actual sounds you are recording, so he or she won't be able to make good judgments about the sound quality.

In a pinch or if you're on location (such as in your hotel room while shooting in Rome), a small, inexpensive headset from a hands-free telephone works pretty well and is easier than trying to hold the phone up to your mouth without blocking the microphone. Buy a telephone headset device that allows you to talk on the phone hands-free. This usually will include a little earpiece and a small microphone. You'll be able to hear the other parties on the line, and they'll hear you speak. You will, of course, also be recording yourself properly through your regular microphone/recording setup. The earpiece is just for communicating with people outside the session. Headsets cost less than $20.

For quality sound and results, you really need a professional telephone interface. The good news? Phone patch interfaces are not prohibitively expensive. The MicTel manufactured by CircuitWerkes (http://www.broadcastboxes.com) is a nifty little box roughly five inches long by two inches high and three inches wide. It's portable and very simple to use with a professional (XLR) connector for your microphone and jacks for input/output, as well as headphones, and it's even a mini-mixer. Best of all, it can run on a nine-volt battery or wall power. Other products include the Comrex TCB1A (http://www.comrex.com) and the Excalibur HC-1, which range in price from $80 to $150. A good source for these telephone interfaces is Broadcast Supply Worldwide (http://www.bswusa.com).

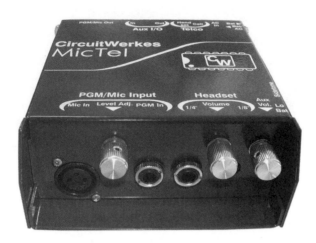

The CircuitWerkes MicTel phone patch interface

One tip, which one of us learned the hard way: Inexpensive interfaces like these utilize your telephone's electronics to work. When you are ready to record, unplug the handset from the telephone and plug it into the interface. Don't try to use a telephone that has the keypad on the handset—that means the electronics are located there rather than on the base. If you do, as you've probably guessed, the moment you unplug the handset, the interface won't have the telephone electronic "guts" to work with, and it will just sit there looking up at you as sweat drips from your brow. So use a more old-fashioned (and certainly not wireless) telephone, and it'll work great.

If you are really handy with a soldering iron, you can even cobble together a decent interface from parts purchased at Radio Shack. Find the circuit you need and the instructions for wiring it up properly on author Jay Rose's Web site (http://www.dplay.com/tutorial/Mac2tel.html). Although he references using this homegrown telephone interface with Macs, the circuit works fine with PCs and mixers.

Exactly how you'll set up your patch will depend on what kind of mixer you have and the way it has been wired. You can save some time and energy by asking or paying a professional to "plumb" your system for a patch. Fundamentally, patches (regular telephone or digital, which we'll discuss shortly) require what's called a *mix minus*. That simply means that as you are recording, you'll hear yourself and the producer in your headphones, and the producer will hear what you are recording on his or her end. But—and this is obviously critical—you won't be recording *them*, only you. Hence, the moniker "mix minus"—it's you, minus the conversation on the phone, recorded.

Integrating the Phone Patch/ISDN Codec into Your Studio

When using a regular telephone phone patch or ISDN digital phone patch, here's how to set up your mix minus.

The only real solution is to use an audio mixer that has an auxiliary bus—essentially a mixer within a mixer. The slang word "bus" simply refers to a way to route or move signals around. Auxiliary buses may also be called *monitor* or *effects* buses, depending on your mixer brand. Many aux buses have a "pre" button, sometimes abbreviated PFL. This simply means the auxiliary bus gets its signal pre-fader, or before the main channel fader affects the volume level.

With the following setup you'll be able to hear both the remote conversation and your performance in your headphones, while simultaneously sending only your voice to the client.

Plug your mic into the mixer as you normally would, and set levels with the channel fader and so forth. Now, take the *output* of the telephone phone patch or ISDN digital telephone's codec and bring it into another channel at the mixer. Don't think we didn't just hear you mutter, "Codec? When did these clowns start talking about photography all of the sudden?" *Codec* is the acronym for code/decode. It functions similarly to a computer modem (which stands for modulator/demodulator). Like your audio interface, a codec takes signals and translates them into information the computer can recognize. Now set a comfortable level for this audio using its channel fader so you can hear the remote site clearly.

Plug the output of the auxiliary bus into the *input* of the phone patch or ISDN codec. On the mixer's auxiliary bus, use the knob that corresponds to your microphone channel only. Turn it up all the way. If you have a pre button, engage it. Keep all other auxiliary knobs off. Next, slowly increase the volume on the auxiliary bus main knob until you're sending the correct level to the phone patch or ISDN codec.

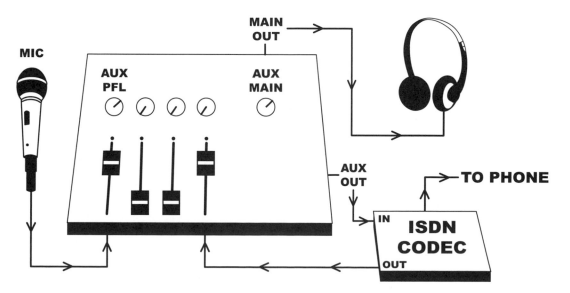

Here's how to hook up the phone patch/ISDN codec to your studio.

The Telos Zephyr Xstream ISDN codec

There are few drawbacks to a traditional phone patch session.

▶ **Audio quality.** Because the bandwidth on a telephone is pretty limited, the producer won't be able to hear every nuance of your stellar performance as clearly as if he or she were actually in the studio with you. Even worse are the sessions when 12 people gather in the conference room and try to listen and direct you via a speaker phone; it's like listening in a canyon.

▶ **Delivery delay.** The second problem is one of time. Now that you've recorded—and they agreed on—the takes you are going to provide, your clients have to sit back and wait. The wait is short if you can quickly send your audio via the Internet, and much longer if you burn a CD and over-night or snail-mail it. For long narrations and documentaries or a session with hundreds of takes, it's often less practical to use the Net for delivery, unless you and your clients have access to ultra-fast T-1 Internet connections.

▶ **Responsibility.** The third drawback to traditional phone patches might sound a little esoteric, but believe us, it's not. When you, the talent, are recording in your home studio for anything other than a simple audition, even with direction and ultimate approval from the client you are playing engineer, producer, and talent. You are guaranteeing that the audio will be usable and broadcast-quality. This is a lot of responsibility, far more than in a "normal" studio setting, where the producer hears all the takes and decides that he or she is happy with your interpretation and the audio's quality and suitability. All you have to do is read the script in time and as directed, sign your contract, and leave. Because of the limitations of regular POTS (sorry, we just had to use that term at least once) telephone lines, you are serving as the producer's "ears" and ensuring that the takes are air-quality.

Is there a way to work from your home studio without the drawbacks of a traditional phone patch? Of course—it's called a digital phone patch, delivered over ISDN digital telephone lines.

ISDN Patches

ISDN is the digital way studios, broadcasters, and actors "send" their voices and images around the world instantly. It's as close to teleportation as we have. ISDN stands for *Integrated Services Digital Network*, but we really don't care, nor do ISDN users have to worry much about a lot of the arcane techno-babble associated with ISDN. Unfortunately, listening to ISDN-savvy performers or engineers can give you severe heartburn and leave you totally intimidated. Discussions of SPIDs, codecs, layers, and BRIs leave us cold too, so we'll make this as simple as we can.

Setting Up the Dial-Up
For two ISDN codecs to communicate with each other, they have to be set up the same. Unlike a regular telephone, where you have no control over how your voice is sent, in a digital world you have way too much control over bits per seconds and scary stuff like that. This could be a problem for voice actors, but it isn't because 99.99 percent of the time, you'll send your voice with both codecs set at Layer 2, Mono 128.

That's the mantra for virtually every session you'll do. When you and the engineer at the other location test the lines (in advance), he or she will almost always say, "Hi, I'm set at L2 (Layer 2), Mono 128," and you'll reply, "Me too." You really don't need to know anything else, and if the remote engineer wants some other setting (highly unlikely) he or she will talk you through changing the setup. Despite all the ways you *could* send data via ISDN, for voice work it's almost always Layer 2 (L2), Mono. When the connection is made you'll hear two little digital-sounding bleeps and marvel at the clarity of the producer's voice in your headphones.

Cost, not technical ability, is the biggest reason few voice talents have discovered the advantages of having an ISDN-equipped studio. Performers who do any amount of promo work for radio or TV stations must have ISDN available in order to compete in that market.

Is the investment worth it? We think so. ISDN almost always more than pays for itself with the increased work opportunities it brings. You really can work globally with your ISDN-equipped studio. Believe it or not, many clients will actually insist on paying you a fee for using your ISDN home studio facilities, as the following true story illustrates.

Harlan: Hello?

Caller: Harlan, it's Joan. Where are you?

I'D JUST DRIVEN HOME FROM A DOWNTOWN CHICAGO STUDIO AND WAS STANDING IN LINE AT THE DEERFIELD POTBELLY SANDWICH SHOP. MY CELL PHONE RANG AT PRECISELY 12:05. SHOUTING OVER THE VERY BAD GUITARIST LABORING IN THE LOFT SPACE ABOVE THE VERY BUSY RESTAURANT—I COULD ONLY ASSUME HE WAS TRYING TO REMOVE THE LAST TRACES OF VARNISH FROM HIS SIX-STRING GUITAR RATHER THAN CREATE ANY SEMBLANCE OF MUSIC—I PRACTICALLY SCREAMED INTO THE PHONE.

Harlan: Potbelly's!

Joan: Downtown?

Harlan: Suburbs!

Joan: McCann-Erickson in Detroit wants you to narrate a DaimlerChrysler film at 1:00. It's a digital patch session. How long will it take you to get downtown?

Harlan: I'd never make it in time.

Joan: I guess they'll have to use their second choice.

Harlan: See if they'll let me ISDN it from my house.

Joan: I'll try....

LESS THAN FIVE MINUTES LATER—LESS TIME THAN IT TOOK TO GET MY TUNA SALAD AND HOT PEPPERS—TAMMY FROM MCCANN-ERICKSON RANG MY CELL PHONE.

Tammy: Hi, Harlan. We're on for a 1:00 session with you. Give me your numbers, and what kind of box do you have?

Harlan: Zephyr, 847-756-4764 and 847-756-4765.

Tammy: Got it. Ron Rose Recording in Southfield will call you. What's your studio fee?

"I LOVE IT WHEN THEY ASK THAT," I THOUGHT.

Harlan: $150

Tammy: That's fine. We'll be bridging to an APT box, so let's test connections at 12:55, okay? Oh, you'll be at L2, Mono 128, right?

RIGHT. AND SO I GOT LUNCH, MADE AN EXTRA HUNDRED AND FIFTY BUCKS, AND MOST IMPORTANT, DIDN'T LOSE THE SESSION TO THEIR SECOND CHOICE—ALL BECAUSE OF ISDN.

Having an ISDN-equipped studio takes you to a new level of professionalism and can even become a profit center, or at least pay its own way. Having ISDN also qualifies you for a number of free Internet listings that allow producers to find digitally-connected talents, such as The Audiobahn (http://www.dplay.com/audiobahn.html), The Digital Dial-Up List (http://www.digifon.com/aboutddl.html), and the Broadcast ISDN User Guide & Directory (http://www.broadcastisdn.net/book.php).

Of course, you'll want to promote your new connectivity to your client list and prospects as well. Let recording engineers know you have ISDN, but make it clear you aren't out to take work from them, because that is the truth. Instead, say you are even more available to them, and when they are in a time crunch or the client forgot to book a voiceover, they now know they can get you on (literally) a moment's notice.

Also, having a home recording studio can become a source of income for you, and making your home studio available to other actors to do ISDN sessions can certainly help pay the monthly costs of your setup and maybe make you a tidy profit as well.

Your local phone company will install special ISDN lines to your home; it's pretty much available anywhere now, and installation is usually around $150. Of course there will be an additional monthly fee of around $40 to $50. Ordering the right setup for audio purposes can be a bit confusing, but in the last few years most telephone companies have become pretty savvy about the needs of voice actors. Essentially, you are simply sending data over the ISDN lines; the fact that it's your dulcet tones is pretty much a moot (not mute) point to them.

You'll get two, not one, ISDN phone numbers installed because this digital connection uses two physical and three logical lines. Why extra lines? To get the bandwidth necessary to send your voice with on-the-air quality to a location anywhere in the world instantly! When you finish an ISDN session it's exactly as if you were face to face with a producer in the studio. The producer has the broadcast-quality takes he or she needs, and you are free to move on to (or dial up to) your next session.

If you have a slow dial-up Internet connection and you don't have or can't get DSL or cable in your area, you can also use your ISDN lines to surf the Net at roughly twice the speed of a 56k modem. Two caveats, though. One, you'll need a special ISDN modem that costs several hundred dollars new, such as those made by 3Com. With the popularity of cable and DSL, however, fewer people use ISDN for Internet connections. We've regularly seen used ISDN modems for sale on eBay for as little as $15! The second caveat is, you'll have to use an Internet Service Provider that has ISDN capability. EarthLink does; AOL doesn't.

Once you've got your numbers (your SPIDS, in ISDN-speak), you'll have to invest in that codec we mentioned. Suffice it to say, this device takes your voice and crams it down the phone lines so it can be uncrammed at the other end by the other locations. Not so fast, though—there are different types of codecs, and they are not compatible. The most popular codec is MPEG, which stands for *Moving Picture Experts Group*. (Yeah, we know we weren't going to get into definitions, but we find this one funny—sounds more like a movie critics club, doesn't it?) Another is APT (*Audio Processing Technology*). Many studios have both of these kinds of codecs, as do a few performers. In general, most voice actors buy MPEG codecs. If you need to "talk" to a studio that only has APT, it's very simple to arrange a bridge. Companies such as Digifon and Ednet provide bridging services for a moderate fee, so the Beta versus VHS/MPEG versus APT debate isn't a big deal. Internationally, MPEG is clearly the most popular.

Buying an ISDN codec isn't cheap; even used they are well over a thousand dollars, and a new codec can cost thousands more depending on its features. You can lease or rent them, though. The CDQ Prima made by Musicam USA (http://www.musicamusa.com) and Telos' Zephyr models (http://www.telos-systems.com) seem to be the most popular. Both companies make portable units as well, such as the Prima RoadRunner (around $3,000).

Portable ISDN codec

Luckily, there are many experts you can talk to about installing ISDN, such as Dave Immer at Digifon. His Web site (http://www.digifon.com) provides a wealth of help and advice as well as products and services to many studios and voiceover actors across the country. He even offers prepackaged voiceover packages with everything you need. He also has complete ISDN line ordering instructions on his Web site and is one of the most helpful and generous people on the planet when it comes to helping even non-clients with ISDN problems. Harlan called him in a panic one day when he just couldn't connect with a studio in Washington, DC.

"What are you using?" Dave asked.

"TELOS Zephyr," Harlan replied, as sweat began to bead on his brow.

"And the client?"

"CDQ Prima."

"Speed dial 19."

"What?"

"Tell your client to push speed dial setting number 19 on the Prima; it's all set up to communicate with your Zephyr. Okay?"

Was it ever! These two codecs instantly communicated.

Ednet (http://www.ednet.net) can also provide help with lines, equipment, and services. If you really want an in-depth education and ISDN resource, check out Dan Kegel's ISDN Web pages (http://www.alumni.caltech.edu/~dank/isdn/index.html). Yeah, we know—just typing in the Web address is intimidating, but this resource is worth the extra keystrokes. Obviously, Mr. Kegel doesn't follow our advice of keeping Web domains simple and easy to remember. But you will, right?

All right, the lines are installed and the codec is plumbed into your recording system with a mix-minus setup similar to the one we used for regular phone patches. (See the sidebar entitled "Integrating the Phone Patch/ISDN Codec into Your Studio" earlier in this chapter.) Now what happens? Well, here are two very important tips for any ISDN session. First, if you haven't "talked" to a particular studio before, *always* test the lines and the setup before the session. Second, remember that the caller pays. It's traditional—if anything in the digital world can be considered traditional—for the client to call the voice performer and arrange and pay for a bridge, if necessary, between incompatible codecs.

The Future on the Net?

Making the investment in ISDN is a big decision, and you can't help but wonder whether this technology, like so many others, might suddenly disappear, and your expensive codec will become a boat anchor. Many actors wonder whether an Internet version of ISDN will become available.

The Internet sends data in packets, not as a continuous stream, and until recently there wasn't any Internet/computer-based codec. Now there is a software program available called AudioTX (http://www.audiotx.com) priced a little under $800, although you have to add other equipment to your computer for it to work, so figure a thousand dollars total.

The downside of this software solution is that your client needs to have the same software setup (or you'd have to bridge connections as we explained earlier—but that adds an additional cost to the session). The fact is, most studios have hardware-based codecs.

It's a pretty good bet, though, that even traditional telephone calls will travel the same information super highway that the Internet does. Voiceover Internet protocol will probably change everything in the telephone business, and many cable Internet companies are going head to head with the telephone companies and their—all together now—POTS lines.

But...

Because the broadcasting industry is slow to buy new equipment when the "old" stuff works just fine (there are plenty of people still recording on magnetic tape), we think the odds are that ISDN will be around for a long, long, time. It has such a strong presence in studios around the globe. In the meantime, AudioTX will solve a problem for a performer living in an isolated area where ISDN is not available, and until the Internet becomes the main method of delivering voice communication.

All right, those are the major advantages of an ISDN-based patch versus a phone patch. From an actor's perspective, an ISDN session is so much simpler—there are no tracks to send later, and you are not responsible for making any audio decisions since the producer is hearing and approving your takes in real time. When you hang up—technically "drop" the line(s)— you're through.

Always Drop Both Lines!

Speaking of dropping lines, one final tip. Since you connect with two telephone lines, you have to hang up or "drop" *both* lines at the end of the session. If you initiated the call and you only drop one line, then...you guessed it, a whopping telephone bill could be coming your way.

Right after Harlan installed his ISDN hookup, he proudly demonstrated the sound quality to his wife, Lesley, by calling up Telos, the manufacturer of his codec. Telos plays music 24 hours a day on ISDN so you can always test your lines and equipment. She was impressed by the sound, but not the $187 phone bill that showed up the next month. Whew! Harlan dropped only one line, leaving the other connected all weekend. That was a very lengthy one-ISDN-line call to Ohio.

In closing, although we promised to not speak in ISDN techno-babble, here's a phrase from an ISDN manual we just can't resist tossing around: "Digital telephone codecs use Psycho-Acoustic Masking to send audio."

One of us, who shall remain nameless, says that means the computer inside your codec analyzes the sound, determines what the most important parts are, and automatically eliminates any sound and data not absolutely necessary. This is the same principle that MP3 works on to squeeze large sound files into space that fits on your MP3 player or iPod.

The other of us, equally nameless, claims Psycho-Acoustic Masking is a patented makeup technique developed by Max Factor for that Jim Carrey flick where he was dancing around with a green face—but you decide.

6 } Painless Promotion

"If you build it, he will come.

If you build what, who will come?

People will come….

They'll turn up your driveway, not knowing for sure why they're doing it."

—*Field of Dreams:* Phillip Alden Robinson/W.P. Kinsella, Universal, 1989

And then again, they might not. Sorry, but it's truth time: That Web site you labored over, that new in-home studio you painstakingly built, that killer new voice demo you just got a couple of thousand dupes of might (and likely will) just lay there. It doesn't have its own legs, and people will not, as a rule, knock down your door and ask for a copy.

The movies not withstanding, just building something—even something terrific—doesn't mean the world will suddenly sit up and take notice. "They" won't magically come to your Web site, book your home studio, or listen to your new cutting-edge voice demo unless you convince them to come, book you, or listen. And to do that, you must promote.

Both of us are big believers in constant, consistent promotion—what Jeffrey calls "ruthless self-promotion" (from his book of the same name). Whether you are selling your voiceover skills or your new studio, your promotion will consist of five basic techniques.

▶ **Direct contact.** When you are talking on the phone, via the talk-back in a recording session, or sitting down with your agent or producer reviewing your new demo, you are making a sales call. Sales calls are how business gets done. And although we'd like to think of ourselves as creative artists (in England they call voiceovers "voice artistes"), the fact is we do have something to sell—our talent. And our talent will help the end client also sell his or her products or service.

▶ **Publicity.** This usually involves articles or mentions in industry and general-interest publications about you, your recent work, or accounts. Many actors, particularly celebrities, have publicists to make sure the press is aware of their every success and to handle any damage control when they fail. The great thing about publicity is that it is (or at least it appears to be) third party. Someone else, not you, talks about your brilliant voiceover career and its triumphs. You can hire PR professionals, of course, but you might be surprised how easy it is to write a brief story about a recent success and send it to one of the trade periodicals. They are very often anxious to use it.

▶ **Direct response.** When you send a promotion directly to prospects, such as a postcard, letter, your latest voice demo, or even an e-mail, it is an example of direct response promotion. This is a one-on-one approach to prospects you feel confident might hire you for voice work. Most actors or their agents invest considerable time in compiling and maintaining a list of potential employers and then send those prospects direct promotions. Your list will most likely start with your present clients and then expand to potential clients that hire voice talent. Often, you'll be able to tell how well a promotion does because your prospects will respond by requesting a demo, audition-ing, or hiring you.

▶ **Advertising.** A more scatter-shot way of promoting is to buy adver-tising. For voiceovers that almost always means print advertising. Buying a print ad—called *space*—in a production periodical is a traditional approach. Advertising hopefully will result in actual bookings, but it has the extra benefit of helping establish and maintain an image of you as a successful performer. The downside to buying ads is that they will reach many non-prospects as well. Therefore, ads are much more expensive than the highly focused and targeted direct response approach. Space advertising is also harder to track than direct response. People rarely tell you they saw your particular ad (unless you ask when they call). Most experts advise that strategic advertising partnered with judicious direct response is a terrific long-term promotional strategy.

► **Advertising specialties.** Many actors find giveaways, such as mouse pads, coffee cups, pencils, and pens, are an effective way to thank a producer for hiring them and serve as a gentle reminder for future bookings. You can have literally thousands of items customized with your name and contact information to leave behind after a session or send out as direct response promotions. The Yellow Pages and the Internet list thousands of companies who offer what some derisively call "trash and trinkets." It's important that any giveaway is of good quality, but not so expensive that you find yourself getting stingy about giving them away or they border on being regarded as bribes. The more your item relates—and is useful—to your client's work, the more successful it will be. Over the years Harlan has found his humorous production calendars and stopwatches to be the most memorable and successful giveaways. Both were unique to the audio production business and useful to clients and potential clients.

Making Your Own (or another Actor's) Killer Voice Demo

Nobody is going to hire you unless you can prove that you have the chops and you can indeed deliver what they need. Therefore, the first, most important task for you is to put together a demo of your voice work.

For voiceovers, the search for the perfect demo is akin to the search for the Holy Grail. More often than not, it's as frustrating as Sancho Panza and Don Quixote pursuing the Impossible Dream. (Wow, those are some mixed metaphors, eh?) Although performing voiceover work is fun, making that first or five hundredth voice demo—well, that's a lot of hard work, often full of worry and heartfelt angst.

There are, of course, people who can make the job easier. From professional voice demo producers to audio engineers who will, for a fee ranging somewhere between reasonable and astronomical, put the whole damn thing together for you. But be forewarned, whether you create your own voice demos in your new home studio, ask for help from an experienced audio producer or engineer, or even pop for one of the big guns, there is never, ever any guarantee that it will "work" and bring you any income.

Killer, cutting-edge, and trendy your new demo may be, full of great sound design it may be, breakthrough it may be, wildly imaginative it may be, expensive it may be…but as the legendary advertising icon David Ogilvy once said, "If it doesn't sell, it isn't creative."

Never forget that the only—*only*—reason for creating a voice demo is to get work. More work. Better work. "Don't confuse selling with art," was the advice of another advertising expert, Jack Taylor. Your demo has to sell you—to your agent or a prospective one, or to an employer, a writer, or a producer. That's it. Your voiceover demo is a selling tool, not unlike a salesman's samples or brochures—you know, the heart and soul of the sales call we talked about. It sells a single product/service—you and your ability to speak. And just like any sales demo, your voice demo must look and sound very good. Very, very good.

So what's the secret? Your demo needs to follow the very basic theatrical structure you studied back in school. Like a play or movie, your demo needs a dramatic arc, complete with a beginning, middle, and end.

▶ **Act One.** How to start? It doesn't matter if you're a working pro with hundreds of actual produced spots from which to choose, or you're young, green, and forced to create your own voice samples. Begin with your "signature" or "money" voice. Always start with the sound you are usually (or most likely to be) hired for. It's sad but nevertheless true that producers listen to only the first few seconds of a voice talent demo. That means you'd better put your most sought-after sound right up front and in their face. You can't hope they'll stick around to hear all the other things you can do. Some will; most won't. Don't take any chances. Lead with a wallop that grabs the not-so-easily impressed and doesn't let go.

▶ **Act Two.** Relax just a little after the thundering overture of the first act. Throw in a character voice or a nice, crisp bit of dialogue to add a little drama to the demo. Don't go too far afield because you have to keep this section brief. Soon it'll be time for:

▶ **Act Three.** You are reaching the end of the arc, the finale, and you want to leave them remembering you for that one particular sound people hire you for over and over again. End your voiceover demo with another example of your signature voice.

This very basic form works, whether you are producing your own voice demo at home, helping create a demo for a fellow actor, or—as we advise—using your home recording equipment to create a rough cut or first draft of your demo that you can then refine with the advice of your agent and the help of a sound design professional.

No Content? No Problem

Years ago, voiceover demos were three or more minutes long and were, in fact, audio resumes. It was considered bad form to put any "created" spots on your reel. Well, times have changed and we voice actors realized that too often the actual spots we did, particularly television commercials, weren't really the right media to showcase our voices. So little by little "created" demos have become the norm. Jeffrey and I, as recording engineer (and guy who often hires voice talent) and voice talent (and guy who often records voice talent), respectively feel that's fine, as long as you don't pretend to have done an actual commercial that someone else has.

What do you do if you hate the stuff you actually have on the air and you are smart enough not to use audition copy for your demo? (You know in your heart of hearts that if the audition copy is any good, it'll end up on 99 other actors' voice demos.) There is a treasure trove of great copy lurking right there in your home. Really? Don't see it? It's underfoot, piled in the bathroom, stacked on your nightstand, and stuffed daily in your mailbox. We're talking about magazines and catalogs. They provide a veritable cornucopia of great voiceover demo copy. With just a touch of rewriting, this material provides fabulous spots for you or for your client's demo. Don't just plagiarize the whole thing, of course—be creative with the copy you find and certainly change it to the first person. Just think of this as another form of recycling.

If you are really smart—or devious—you'll be careful *not* to mention the name of the product in your created copy. This has two benefits. One, no one will ever accuse you of claiming to do a commercial you didn't actually do. And two, no producer-type hearing your demo will worry that you've already done a spot for a competitor. (That's a surefire way not to get hired!) Pick intriguing copy that showcases you, not the product. Eliminating the product's name helps you concentrate on demonstrating your own unique way with words. As for using real spots for your demo, that's the best scenario of all, of course. Unfortunately, it's often difficult to get a copy of your work. You can ask if you can get a dub of something you've just recorded as you are about to leave a studio. Naturally, offer to pay for the copy. But it might be days or even weeks before the final mix is finished, approved, and on the air. All too often the promised spot simply never shows up. On the other hand, if you wait and try to obtain a copy after the fact, you'll spend hours tracking down the producer just to get permission, and then you might spend quite a sum of money at the recording studio if they have to restore the recorded elements onto a computer just to make your solitary dub.

This is where having your home studio and basic computer skills can really pay off. Now when you're leaving the studio—assuming the producer gives you permission—simply ask the audio engineer to send you an MP3 when the spot is finished and approved. Hand him or her your card (you *do* have business cards, right?) with your e-mail address on it (your card *does* have your e-mail address, right?), and when you get the MP3 you can plop it into your audio software and paste it into your new demo. You might have to remind the engineer—strike that, you *will* have to remind the engineer—once or twice, but do it in a fun, low-key way and eventually he or she will send over the spot. What the heck, even those conversations are in fact—you guessed it—sales calls!

How Long Should a Great Voice Demo Be?

Let's avoid any politically incorrect, tacky debate over whether length matters. Let's just say that your demo should be...well...long enough. But not too long. Putting an arbitrary time limit on it is fruitless. It's really more about how much variety you have to show and how long the listener *perceives* the demo to be.

Jeffrey received a voiceover demo not long ago that was so full of super-fast quick cuts that he swore it must have been three or four minutes in length. The performer had crammed 15 different spots into—ready?—one minute and 25 seconds! It gave Jeffrey a headache, was useless as a casting tool, and even after listening to it again and again, *it seemed to go on forever.*

Short and simple should be your guidelines. Don't worry about making a "killer" or "breakthrough" demo. Always remember that your goal is to present a product—you or your client—in the best possible light. Make sure your demo gives an accurate representation of your talent in a way that works. And that means sells!

All about Home Studio Auditions

Generally, talent agents and casting directors are the portals for auditions, although you might find producers sending you auditions directly. Be careful when you record these at home and return them via e-mail. The moment you click Send, your work is out of your control. If you've recorded at air quality, your audition could end up on the air or even on someone's Web site! You wouldn't get paid and you might have violated your union and agent obligations.

Depending on whether you live and work in a larger or smaller market, you might find an agent a necessity to even get auditions. Getting representation is often difficult, even for seasoned professional voiceovers. Agents have their stable of talent and, as good as you may be, they might simply have too many other performers already in your category. Newcomers also find it difficult to find an agent willing to take a chance on them. Luckily, there some strategies that do work, which Harlan discusses at length in his book *VO: Tales and Techniques of a Voiceover Actor.*

If you have representation, it is wise to send all your auditions via your agent for protection. Alternatively, you can use this little trick: Alter the copy. Intentionally transpose a few words or even mispronounce them so the audition can't become the real thing. A few years back, an agent who represents celebrity voiceovers discovered he'd been ripped off and his client's auditions were going on the air. To prevent this from happening again, he started recording a 60-Hz hum tone very faintly in the background! You can do the same thing with your computer-based recording software. You could even insert random blips and beeps to further prevent the piracy of your auditions.

A huge benefit of recording the auditions your agent or a casting director e-mails, faxes, or sends to you to record at home is that it's so much easier and faster than physically going to your agent's office to record in his or her sound booth. Today your audition will be converted to an MP3 and e-mailed to the producer regardless of where you recorded it. Also, there are some psychological benefits to recording at home. The waiting rooms at most agent's and casting director's offices are wall to wall with actors. This can be a bit intimidating if you're relatively new to the world of cattle calls. More importantly, everyone is in a hurry to get you in and out, and too often you just don't get a chance to experiment with your reading. Nine times out of ten you are halfway home when the right reading dawns on you. But by then, it's too late. Auditioning in your home studio provides a quiet oasis in which you can record as many takes as you like, listen to them, and then choose the one or two you feel are your strongest.

Plus you have control over the sound of your audition. More than likely, the equipment you own now (or soon will) is as good and often far better than your agent's equipment. Using your computer you can clean up your takes, perhaps adding a touch of EQ or compression so they stand out. Don't go overboard with these tricks. Your tracks will be sent along with all the other actors' takes, so they can't sound *too* different. But, life being life, the absolute best take will inevitably have a tiny mouth noise in it or a big honking breath sound. Those flaws would stay in the audition if it was recorded anywhere else, but when you record and edit at home, you can zoom in on the waveform and surgically remove the mouth noise and delete that big honking breath just as those little errors would be treated in a professional studio if you were actually doing the session for real.

Promoting Your New Facilities to Clients

Of course you'll want to let your clients, especially the cash-strapped ones, know that you've invested in home recording facilities. Particularly for non-broadcast, "industrial" clients, being able to toss in the studio often will mean the difference between demanding the professional fee you deserve and losing the gig to a discount voiceover.

How do you get the word out?

▶ **Promotional blurbs.** In addition to calling and talking up your new facility, also write a brief blurb that promotes it. Use this blurb on everything you have printed—business cards, demo CD labels, ads, postcards, your Web site, your e-mail signature, and so forth. Try something like this:

Joe Blow has a fully-equipped, all-digital project studio (sounds so much hipper than home studio, doesn't it?) with telephone and ISDN audio patches.

There's no reason to go into your laundry list of the geeky-gear we convinced you to buy, but you should include your ISDN numbers (assuming you have them) on all your stuff, along with your voice and fax telephone numbers. Don't forget to include your e-mail address and Web site URL, too.

▶ **Web promotion**. Brag a bit about your state-of-the-art recording facilities on your Web site and in your e-mail signature. (See Chapter 7, "Untangling the World Wide Web," for details.) Banner ads can also be effective. To promote his other book, *VO: Tales and Techniques of a Voiceover Actor*, Harlan had a banner ad created. The animated ad features three rotating messages: "Finally a book about voiceovers that's almost as much fun as performing them!" "Great stories, great advice," and "Wanna-be, newcomer, or old pro, you'll love it." Clicking the banner takes you to his Web site, with complete ordering instructions for the book and, of course, his voice demo.

Here's an example Web banner used by Harlan.

A number of Web sites were willing to trade space. For example, Harlan put a link to Canada's Commercial Voices site, where he has voice demos, and they were willing to include his banner ad on their site. You should work to get similar reciprocal deals. The cost is free or minimal, and the potential is quite large.

▶ **Traditional direct mail.** You should also use low-tech means to promote your high-tech products and services, such as your home-based project studio, Web site, and perhaps voice-demo producing skills. From a cost effectiveness standpoint, it's hard to beat good old-fashioned postcards. And Internet-based e-cards are even less expensive because you save a bundle on postage.

For the traditional route, start at Modern Postcard (http://www.modernpostcard.com). Their quality and service are tough to beat, as are their prices. They print your full-color postcard along with hundreds of others on huge presses. Bottom line? You can get a thousand cards for $165—that's only 16 cents apiece, in case you didn't want to do the math yourself. Another inexpensive source is Vista Print (http://www.vistaprint.com). Both companies can also mail your cards for you; you only need to supply a computer-created address list.

If you have artistic talent or a pro designer you work with, you can send digital artwork to be printed. Complete specifications are on the site. You can also design from scratch on either company's Web site. There are stock photos and various typefaces available from which you can choose.

► **Internet direct mail.** A higher-tech, lower-cost option is to send electronic postcards. iBuilder (http://www.verticalresponse.com) is one of hundreds of companies that can help you design an e-card and send it on to your list of clients and prospects. Using e-cards assumes you have the e-mail addresses you need already. Because there is no postage or physical printing expense, your cost is less than a tenth of that for traditional postcards.

For example, the cost per thousand e-cards with iBuilder is only $15. Does an e-card have the same impact as an open-the-mailbox-hold-in-your-hand postcard? We certainly don't know for sure, so maybe you'll want to try both. At those prices, why not?

Do I Really Want to Promote My Home Studio?

If all you want to do is edit your own demos and audition from home, we'll write you a permission slip to show to the ever-present hall monitors, saying you are free not to promote your studio. Remember, they are not those monitors we told you to go out and buy earlier in the book. However, if you've invested in phone patch and ISDN equipment, you want to produce voice demos for other actors, you have clients with a limited budget who need talent that comes complete with recording facilities, or you are willing (perhaps anxious) to rent out your facility to other actors, you must promote what you can do.

Ah, but won't "real" recording studios get mad? Studios are well aware that it's imperative for voiceovers to have their own facilities at home. Your goal then, since studios often influence casting decisions, is to make sure you partner—rather than compete—with them. For example, just a few days after Harlan got his ISDN codec he mentioned it to Bob Benson, a Chicago audio engineer. Bob scowled a little and Harlan quickly assured him, "Hey, I'm not going into competition with you guys. This is for the real low-end clients who never come here anyway and for the out-of-towners who just need simple voiceover tracks instantly and..."

"...and never come here anyway," Bob finished for him.

"Besides," Harlan added, "I'm now available to you 24/7, in the unlikely event you need a last-minute VO!"

The next night at 10:30 PM, unlikely turned out to be likely when Bob Benson called Harlan at home. "You awake?"

"I'm not that old," Harlan replied.

"Look, the producer forgot he needed the mandatories recorded for tomorrow. You know: 'McDonald's is an equal-opportunity employer' kind of stuff. Give me your ISDN numbers."

Ten minutes later, Harlan was recording six McDonald's commercials, all because he'd mentioned casually and in a non-threatening way that he had ISDN, a home studio, and most important, that those facts might be beneficial to the engineer.

And one more thing. Jeffrey, despite owning a money-making professional recording studio, still prefers to hire talent who can do it themselves. He feels it's more cost effective to drop in finished tracks than to record and edit them himself. So whether the session is via ISDN or e-mailed MP3s, VOs and home studios go together well!

Promoting Your New Facilities and Abilities to Other Actors

If you've decided to offer your services and recording facilities to other actors for sessions, auditions, or as a producer of talent demos, you'll need to promote to them, too. Word of mouth will always be your best advertising. Tell everybody about what you do and make sure you include your complete contact information on every piece that leaves your studio—letters, e-mail, CD labels, and so on.

One actor we know with a home studio landed a regular gig recording an actress at his place. Their mutual agent had casually mentioned that the actress was going to lose a monthly narration job for an out-of-town client because of the high costs of a full-fledged Chicago studio. "What do they need?" asked the studio owner.

"Just straight tracks," she replied. "They edit and assemble them at their AV department."

"I can do that."

"Yeah, but they direct over a phone patch."

"I can do that."

And so he did, and he is making a nice monthly fee from his home studio without even opening his mouth other than to say, "We're rolling on track one."

What kinds of promotions should you consider?

▶ **Printed promotions.** You'll want to at least print up some business cards listing your services and facilities. You can easily make these on your home computer (ah, another way those computer skills pay off!) using Avery's Clean Edge Business Card stock (http://www.avery.com). A better alternative, especially for color cards, might be to use an online printer such as Printing For Less (http://www.printingforless.com).

Another printed material you should consider is an inexpensive one-page flyer or a more detailed brochure, such as a single piece of paper folded into thirds. Put a picture on the cover with a good headline. Plaster the panel that folds behind the cover with glowing testimonials from all your happy customers. Detail what you offer on the inside three panels. Use the back panel for your contact information. This brochure could even be a self mailer.

▶ **Bulletin boards.** Believe it or not, you can get a lot of free promotion by posting your business card, flyer, and/or brochure on bulletin boards! Actor-oriented bookstores, such as the Drama Bookstore in New York, Soliloquy in Chicago, or Samuel French in LA all have them, as do most performing union offices. Your agent might also have a spot where you can put your material for other actors to see. Consider posting your promotional materials on bulletin boards at local colleges and universities, too.

▶ **Advertising.** You can also purchase advertising in performer-oriented periodicals such as *Backstage*, *Variety*, *Screen*, *Audition News*, *PerformInk*, or Los Angeles' *The Voice Over Resource Guide*, which comes out in print and on the Web and is expanding to markets outside of LA. See the Resources appendix at the conclusion of this book for contact information. Your ad might be a small, simple classified announcement or a larger—and more costly—display advertisement. Which you choose depends on your budget. It's better to place a smaller ad consistently than to empty the piggy bank on one larger ad that only runs once.

Expert Help

Stop by any bookstore or local library and you'll find a staff of experts on advertising and promotion waiting for you in the form of countless (and often great) books available. We both like all of the books in the *Guerrilla Marketing* series. *The Guerrilla Marketing Handbook*, for example, is practical, thought-provoking, and aimed at individuals who sell to other individuals—like us.

Harlan feels you should definitely read Jeffrey's other books, *Ruthless Self-Promotion in the Music Industry* and *Profiting from Your Music and Sound Project Studio.* Even though they are aimed at music business promotion rather than voiceover work, they contain many tips and techniques you can use to promote your new studio facilities and voiceover talent. When reached for comment, Jeffrey did not disagree.

Home Studio, Legal, and Logistic Concerns

Another reality check. If you are having clients come to your home or apartment to record or create demos, check your homeowner's or apartment-dweller's insurance policy. Should someone get injured in your home, you want to be sure you are properly covered. Insurance for your home studio, in this instance, should be very reasonable, so even if you get a rider to your normal insurance policy, it shouldn't be cost-prohibitive. Call your insurance agent and explain the situation.

Your apartment building, condo, homeowner's association, or town might have strict zoning laws about conducting business in a residential area. Again, do a bit of homework before you begin your "home work." Don't say we didn't warn you!

Keep good records of the deductible business expenses for your home-based studio and also all the income it makes. Our pals at the Internal Revenue Service seem to find this stuff important—'nuff said.

Finally, if you have a significant other or some rugrats, cats, or dogs, consider the impact of having strangers trooping into your home or apartment to record with you. Make sure your family members are all cool with this invasion of their privacy

Now You've Built It and They Will Come!

Like so many things about life, and in particular the life we've chosen as performers, we have to trust that good things will happen to us if we prepare well, hone our craft, invest in the right tools and training, and simply hang in there. Building your own home studio and learning the basic art of recording will—believe us—pay huge dividends in the long run, but it does take a giant leap of faith to invest in the equipment and spend the time necessary to learn to use it well.

Sometime hopefully in the not-too-distant future, you'll look at your home recording studio setup and think, "How did I ever get along without this?" and "This was the smartest thing I ever did!"

Be confident that eventually the world will discover you, your home studio, and your unique abilities as an actor, regardless of whether you are trodding the boards or working the mike. Speaking of discoveries, did you know that Ben Affleck and Matt Damon both appeared in *Field of Dreams*? Don't ruin your eyes squinting at the credits as they roll by at breakneck speed on your TV, though—at the time they were just two more uncredited extras.

7 } Untangling the World Wide Web

Video	Audio
	Narrator:
Fade in: Dot-com executives zooming down Highway 1 in convertible Bentley	The World Wide Web: Many view it as the Gold Rush of the twenty-first century…
Dissolve to: Computer screen, banner ad after banner ad pops up until the screen is full	…while others think a comparison to the lawless days of the wild, wild West is more apt.
Cut to: Still of ecstatic yuppie holding a fan of ten-thousand-dollar bills	Your view is probably tempered by how much you made…
Dissolve to: Still of large family living in a double-wide	…or lost when the dot-com bubble burst…
ECU: Businessman with tear rolling down his cheek; pull back to reveal shuttered bookstore	…and whether your industry has been helped or hurt by this new form of commerce.
B-Roll: 1940s family sitting in the living room in the glow of the Philco console radio, mom knitting, dad reading a book, the children playing Monopoly	Whatever your answer, there's no doubt that things will never be quite the same again.

The Internet and the Voiceover Actor: A Practically Perfect Love Story

The Internet has changed the world of voiceovers in profound ways.
Voice actors can live almost anywhere there is a reasonably high-speed

connection to the Web, and they can e-mail their performances anywhere in the world. You can surf the Web looking for employment and, as more and more sites add audio, actually find new voice work.

This love story does have a few drawbacks. Our new connectivity has created a new competitiveness. Now, no matter where you hang your headphones, you are competing with the best of the best across the country. We've all invaded each other's space to some degree, but that's hopefully offset by the increased opportunities for everyone. More importantly, the Internet offers us a solution to one of the most costly and time-consuming tasks we face in our neverending quest to find work—distribution of our voice demos.

No matter how great your voice demo is (and how current, now that you'll be able to update it regularly in your own home studio), there is the overwhelming job of getting it into the hands of potential employers. Paying to get CDs professionally duplicated is really reasonable today from suppliers such as Disc Makers (http://www.discmakers.com) or Evatone (http://www.eva-tone.com). However, even the best deal for a thousand CDs in full-color cardboard jackets will still cost you around a thousand dollars!

Even if you decide to take the cheapskate route and burn CDs at home, duplication and distribution can quickly eat up your savings as you start adding up all the costs. Blank CDs are inexpensive, but don't forget about that 20-cent label, the jewel case, the 70 cents for that padded envelope to mail it in, and the biggie—postage.

You could deliver them yourself to nearby prospects, but is that the best use of your time? And what if—and you *know* this is going to happen—you get a parking ticket? To make matters worse, resign yourself to this fact: Most of the demos you send out or drop off end up in, as both our fathers used to say, the circular file.

Enter the Internet. Now you can upload your current demo(s) to your agent's Web site, many free and fee-based voice talent sites, or, best yet, your own Web site. That's right, with your own little bit of cyberspace, you can officially become a virtual voiceover.

Audio Sites

There are essentially two destinations for your virtual voice demo—your agent(s) and independent sites.

▶   **Agents.** More than likely your agent has a "House CD sampler" and an Internet Web site where prospective employers can hear you and other talent he or she represents. Often there is a small charge to be included. It's well worth it. Most agents ask that you limit your demo to around a minute in length. Also, they might want several different types of demos, for example a commercial demo, a character voice, and a narration or documentary version. Assemble these at home, get input from and tweak them with a pro audio engineer, and prepare them by converting the finished demos to Real Audio, MP3, or whatever format(s) your agent wants. Sometimes they'll just want a CD (usually without any compression or other audio tricks—we'll explain those in Chapter 8, "Advanced Techniques"—and they'll have their audio-savvy Webmaster prepare your track samples for the site.

▶   **Independents.** There are a number of independent voice-casting audio sites on which you can also put your demo. Most charge a fee; others are free. Fee-based sites include the United States de facto standard, voicebank.net (http://www.voicebank.net), or the excellent Canada-based Commercial Voices (http://www.commercialvoices.com). Voiceartist.com (http://www.voiceartist.com) is free as long as you put a reciprocal link from your Web site to theirs. On the other hand, VoiceHunter.com (http://www. voicehunter.com) provides a free name-only listing, but charges a yearly fee to have your actual voice demos on their site. ShowBiz.com (http://www.show-biz.com) provides totally free listings, but there is no way to post your audio demos. Voices 123 (http://www.voices123.com) has various levels of membership with increasing fees. The bottom line is that you pay for the privilege of auditioning and then bid—like on eBay—for the amount you'd be willing to take for the job once you land it. Naturally, union performers can't and won't participate in this free-for-all auction scheme, and you have to decide whether that's the way you want to pursue your VO career over the long term.

You could end up spending a lot of money to be on the hundreds of talent sites on the Web. Our advice? Go slow. Since most of these sites list their talent roster, talk to at least a few of their other performers to see whether they are happy with the service. No site can ever guarantee that you'll get work, but you're betting that the exposure will at least result in some additional bookings.

A serious word of warning: Harlan once registered on a voiceover site which hosted his demos for free. Why not, he figured. A year later a mundane-looking e-mail arrived at harlanhogan.com, asking him to update his information and requesting a credit card number. Whaaaaat?

The missive went on to explain that the site was going to charge a small fee from now on, *but* they had great news! Harlan and the other voice talents would now be exposed to sixteen million likely prospects every day for a pittance, just one tenth of a cent per prospect!

Aside from the fact that there simply aren't sixteen million prospective employers of voice talent in the whole wide world, even if the site could actually reach sixteen million people a day, there's the problem of the math that even a number-challenged individual like Harlan could fathom.

16,000,000 × .001 = $16,000

When Harlan e-mailed the purveyors of this wonderful opportunity to see whether his figures were right, they were quick to thank him for their faulty math. In fact, the offer was supposed to read sixteen million prospects at one tenth of a cent *per month*! Even if the site could reach sixteen million people a *year*, Harlan decided to spend his spare $192,000 elsewhere, like on esoteric microphones and sending his and his dear friend Jeffrey's children to the finest universities money could buy.

A Domain of Your Own

Nice as it is to be on your agent's site and on several of the group casting services, there is nothing like your own space to really showcase your talents. Best of all, none of your voiceover competition will be nearby. The first step is to secure a domain name, such as joeblow.com or—if you like a more obtuse Web presence—greatvoice.com. Unfortunately, we already have a small problem here because joeblow.com is a T-shirt company, and voiceover actress Susan Berkley owns greatvoice.com. Not to worry, though—in the last few years many other extensions have joined the ubiquitous dot-com, so you might still be able to buy joeblow.tv, although Susan was smart enough to also acquire the moniker greatvoice.biz. However, greatvoice.tv was still available as of this writing.

Wonder if your favorite name is available? The easiest way to find out is to simply do what we just did in the example. We typed www.greatvoice. tv into an Internet browser. Guess what? A page popped up, telling us that it was available for $50 a year and that we could buy it instantly with a credit card. There are many domain name companies out there, but we prefer the largest: Network Solutions (http://www.networksolutions.com). For a very reasonable yearly fee you can establish your own domain presence on the World Wide Web. Consider your domain name an inexpensive and—assuming you pay the annual fee—permanent address on the Net.

As we mentioned, if you know that people frequently misspell your name, you might want to buy similar domain names.

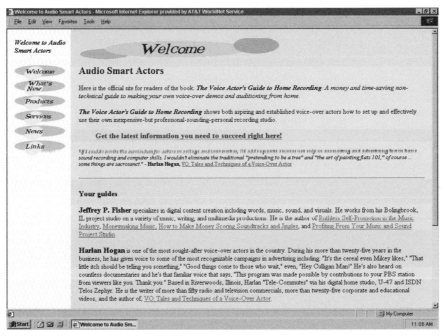

Audio Smart Actors (http://www.audiosmartactors.com) is our Web site designed to support this book. Check it for updates and more information regularly.

Dedicated Web Hosting

More than likely you already have an Internet Service Provider (ISP), such as AOL, EarthLink, or Comcast, that you use to get your e-mail and surf the Web. Many ISPs include a low-cost or no-cost personal Web page. These generally won't work well for promoting your talent and making your demos available to potential clients. Most free sites don't give you enough cyberspace to contain your large audio files—and even if they do, your prospective customers will have to find you by passing through their portal. In plain speak, you want to be able to say, "Click on www. myname.tv to hear my latest voice demo," not ask them to find you at www. earthlink.net.johnnydoe/~html/com.index/funny.ihavetogotosomucheffort_/ tofindthisvoice.htm or something equally bizarre.

So you really need a Web hosting service whose whole business is maintaining Web pages like yours. Yes this will be an additional cost, but it's well worth it. You won't be at the mercy of any one ISP or even a Web-hosting company. If you want or need to change, you can transfer your address to a new provider!

Jeffrey learned this the hard way when his ISP of 10 years went belly up and left him stranded without a place for his Web site. He quickly had to find another home and another domain. Unfortunately, anybody who typed in his old Web address would get the dreaded 404: Page Not Found error. Thankfully, all is well now at www.jeffreypfisher.com.

Network Solutions, the same people who can provide your domain name, offers Web hosting for less than $50 a year. Others, such as Pair Networks (http://www.pair.com) and ADDR.com (http://www.addr.com), offer similar competitive rates based on your specific needs. HostIndex (http://www.hostindex.com) ranks the top Web-hosting companies each month as a free service to help you choose a company that's right for you. Alternatively, try Web Hosting Ratings (http://www.webhostingratings.com).

Another advantage of using a Web-hosting service is FTP. No, that's not the stuff you put in your oil to make your car run smoother. File Transfer Protocol is a necessity for really big audio files.

You can send auditions and short audio selections to clients, prospects, and your agent via regular e-mail. However, most e-mail programs (and ISPs) have limits on the size of files you can send and receive, usually somewhere between two to four megabytes. AOL, for instance, limits attached files to just one megabyte. In plain English, that's far less than a minute of CD-quality audio (in case you forgot, that's five megabytes per minute of mono). Even files you've compressed to MP3 are rather large (about one megabyte per minute). So, should you want to send a long narration or many takes to a client, it's likely that his or her ISP and/or e-mail program will reject the attachment as too large.

Using one of the many free or low-cost FTP programs available, such as BitBeamer or SmartFTP, you can transfer the large audio files to your own Web site. Then, have your client download them at their leisure. As an added bonus, you get your client to visit your Web site once again, and that's not a bad thing, is it?

There's more information about preparing your files for Web encoding in the "Preparing Your Files for Encoding" section later in this chapter.

Do-It-Yourself Web Design

Now you have your domain name ready, great audio prepared, and a Web-hosting company set up. How are you going to design a good-looking, practical, and useful Web site?

First, what should you include on your Web site? We like to think of our sites as cyberstores that sell services (and products, if they apply). So, include your best promotional material, lists of projects and clients you've worked for, articles by and about you, pictures, audio and video samples, your demo, and anything else you feel is important. Of course, your full contact information should be prominent.

As you start to plan your site, think about what you need. You want to present your best image, not just an endless ad. Visit a few other voice-actor Web sites and see how they are using the Web. Apply what you learn to your site. Plot out your pages on paper first, and use those to design your site or give them to your professional designer to use.

Update your pages regularly and check them for mistakes and any links to other resources that don't work, perhaps because they are out of date. Consider providing some extra value on your site, "freebies" if you will, such as information, samples, useful tips, links, and the like. This works in two ways. One, you give useful information and resources to people visiting your site, which makes them want to return regularly to see what's new. Two, you have a reason to promote your site when you do in fact add something new. Again, that drives traffic to your little corner of cyberspace.

Second, you need to physically put together the site. If you're lucky, you've got friends or relatives conversant with otherworldly languages such as Hypertext Markup Language (HTML), the language of the Web. If not, and you feel fairly comfortable with computers and basic design, programs such as Microsoft FrontPage, Adobe Go Live, or Macromedia Dreamweaver can help you design and set up your site.

These programs all use a non-technical approach called WYSIWYG. "Wizzywig" is the technical name for the toupee worn by Frank Morgan as Professor Marvel in the *Wizard of Oz* and the equally impressive geek acronym meaning "What You See Is What You Get." Simply put, as you lay out your Web pages in these programs, you simply design something that looks good to you and voila! What you see on your computer is what others will see when they visit your site. Wizzywig!

But assuming you don't have the time or inclination to learn yet another new skill, or you want a state-of-the-art-gee-whiz Web site, you have two choices: Buy a prefab Web site or hire a professional, such as our friend, Warren King. Prefab sites take care of all the design, but you must still supply the content. Usually you are left to maintain the Web site yourself. Again, running a prefab site requires you to be rather Web savvy. Alternatively, the prefab Web site creators will gladly charge you a fee to customize the design. Therefore, we suggest simply hiring a Webmaster to design and maintain your Web presence.

Your E-Mail John Hancock

Make sure you include an e-mail signature that accompanies all of your outgoing messages. This tagline should include your name, phone number, e-mail address, and Web site address. Consider also adding a short promotional message, too. This is a non-intrusive, non-obnoxious little ad for you and your services. Say something like, "Be sure to visit www.yourdomainnamehere.com to hear my latest voice demos and see pictures of my ISDN-equipped project studio!" To make the Web address a clickable link, type its *full* address (its full Uniform Resource Locator, or its URL), such as http://www. audiosmartactors.com. Refer to your e-mail documentation for details on setting up your signature.

Jeffrey uses a freeware program called Pegasus Mail (http://www.pmail.com) that accommodates multiple signatures. You can write different versions for specific situations and choose the appropriate signature to accompany your message. Pegasus also supports mailing lists, with which you can send the same e-mail to hundreds of people at once.

Harlan, never known for proper penmanship, just tries to sign his e-mails with a black felt marker directly on his computer monitor, resulting in hours of painstaking cleaning every night and nasty smudges throughout his house.

Professional Web Design

Somewhere in the rolling hills of Massachusetts (actually somewhere in Shrewsbury, Massachusetts), a soft-spoken man is sitting surrounded by eight different computers. Warren King is spending this evening, like many others, checking the Web sites he has designed to see that they look and sound right on every kind of "box," from the slowest to the fastest, regardless of the make, model, color, or condition. It's this attention to detail that keeps Warren and other Web designers like him in demand. This is the kind of minute, detailed work that many people with Web sites (and either no time or no technical ability) appreciate. Warren King is the consummate Web design professional, and one you'd be lucky to find.

We asked him what advice he has for the average voiceover who feels comfortable using his or her home studio, recording auditions, saving tracks as .wav files or converting to MP3, and who now is thinking about a Web presence.

Warren: We can do amazing things on a Web site today, but they only make sense if they sell your product—in this case, you. First of all, the cost of your own Web site is not terribly expensive. Depending on how many features you need or want, it will cost somewhere between six dollars and 50 dollars a month. You can do your own design, of course, if all you want to do is create a basic informational page and put a link to your voice demos. The question is whether you have the time or desire to learn. Otherwise, pay a professional.

Jeffrey and Harlan: Do all Web designers know how to do audio?

Warren: There's nothing unique about doing audio anymore. Any Web-hosting company can accommodate Real Audio, Windows Media, Flash, and MP3. A few years ago it was tricky, but now that part is easy since you no longer need any special software to stream your audio. You see, HTTP...

Harlan: Just when we said he wouldn't talk in Web-tongues, he sneaks in "HTTP."

Jeffrey: Shhhhhh!

Warren: HTTP, or Hypertext Transfer Protocol, is used by all Web servers today. It provides up to four or five simultaneous streams of audio at a time. All you have to do is put your audio files on your server and then create a link to them from your Web page.

Harlan: Sounds suspiciously like that's easier said than done.

Warren: Truthfully, it's easier to do than to explain. Technically speaking, it's not at all difficult. I think really good and good-looking design on your Web site is the more important issue. Your site should look professional. It is, after all, a reflection of you. You want any prospective voice clients to have the impression that you are the real thing—that it's not risky to book this person because you are obviously a pro, based on the quality look of your site and, of course, the great sound of your demos.

Jeffrey and Harlan: Okay, so you've finished your demos and posted one or two basic pages in cyberspace. You know prospective employers are out there using the search engines like Yahoo!, Google, and AltaVista to find voice talent. How do you get them to find and visit your site?

Warren: That's the million-dollar question. And the most debated. There are companies online who claim that for a mere $250 a month, they'll guarantee your site will be in the top ten on all the search engines. However, they can't ever prove it because the whole point is illogical. How can all the people they sign on be in the top ten?

You don't need to spend lots of money to get a good ranking in the search engines; just do a couple of things yourself. First, make your pages relevant to what you are doing, concentrate on what you do best, and keep the pages *short* because they rank better. Second, submit your pages to the top search companies whenever you make changes to them.

Jeffrey and Harlan: How?

Warren: On the major search engine sites, you'll find instructions on how to submit your pages. Once you are on the important search engines, they will automatically send their Web-bots out to your site regularly and register any changes.

Harlan: Web-bots—I think George Jetson had one of those that did all the housework.

Jeffrey: Try Rosie the Robot, Harlan.

Harlan: I knew that.

Jeffrey: Warren, is it worth paying a fee to the search engines to be higher up in the listings?

Warren: I don't think it's worth the money.

Jeffrey: Doesn't Yahoo! make you pay to be in their directory?

Warren: Many people feel that it's worth it, although a Yahoo! search will still show Web matches from Google's search engines right after their listings. If you do decide to pay Yahoo! for a listing, *make sure* your site is up and running before you apply. Have no "under construction" pages or links that don't work on your site. The Yahoo! fee is technically for "expediting" your submission—and they can and will reject sites that are not ready, *and* still keep your money.

Harlan: I keep hearing about keywords you need to somehow work into your site so you'll show up early in the Web search engines.

Warren: Choosing the right keywords is both an art and a science because the search engines change the rules of the game constantly. I'd suggest checking out a fascinating (and free) site, http://www.selfpromotion.com, for a post-graduate course in how and why search engines work and what keywords you need to use so you rank higher. You need to not only discover the exact words your potential clients are using to find talent like you, you need to find out what words your prospects are using to find you that your competition is *not* using!

Don't get too hung up on ranking highly in the search engines, though. The fact is, most of the traffic at your site will come from traditional promotion rather than Internet searches. So don't forget to include other simple, traditional promotional ideas, such as postcards and ads.

Put your Web site address on everything—business cards, demo CDs—and include it as a signature on your e-mail. You might consider designing a banner ad as well, if you know other sites—even other actors' sites—that might use them in reciprocity with your Web site.

Jeffrey and Harlan: So in general, you recommend pretty low-tech methods to get people to your high-tech site?

Warren: Absolutely. And assuming you keep some kind of database—a list of customers and prospects—begin, if you haven't already, getting their e-mail addresses. Then you can do regular targeted promotions without the expense of traditional snail-mail. In a few minutes and with a few keystrokes, you can let people know what you are currently doing, and hopefully get them to visit your site to learn more about your talent and hire you for their next project.

Jeffrey and Harlan: Thanks, Warren, and don't stay up too late playing with your computers.

Warren: You're welcome, and you know I will.

Getting Your Voice Web-Ready

Posting your demo, auditions, or other sound clips on the Web is an effective way to let people hear what you can do. Sometimes you also need to prepare your tracks to e-mail to distant clients. Here's the skinny on getting the best sound using the popular Web formats.

As you know, an uncompressed digital file is large, about five megabytes per minute in mono. That's way too big to e-mail efficiently. You need a way to reduce the file size or compress it in some way while still keeping the quality high. There are essentially three main formats for the Web: Real Media, Windows Media, and MP3. All of these are lossy compression formats. This means they lose certain "unnecessary" sounds by using special psycho-acoustic encoders and therefore can make the file size smaller while maintaining reasonable fidelity. For example, the typical 128 Kbps MP3 compresses the audio 11:1, which is a reasonable size that still provides decent quality.

No matter which format you need, select the highest-quality encoding you can, depending on your needs. You don't want to have huge files out there which can take forever to download on a dial-up Internet connection. However, you don't want to send crummy-sounding files that can hurt your chances at landing any work. Strike a balance between performance and file size. For Real Media, choose 100 Kbps audio as a minimum. For Windows Media or MP3, 128 Kbps is ideal.

▶ **Real Media.** One of the original Web audio formats, their compression algorithms are impressive, especially for audio. And you can stream the audio from your Web site easily. Encoding your file to the Real Media format requires using their production tools, called Real Media Producer (http://www.realnetworks.com/products/producer). Alternatively, some audio software, such as the Sound Forge application, lets you save your uncompressed files in the Real Media format, ready for Web posting.

▶ **Windows Media.** This is from the folks in Redmond, Washington and goes head to head with Real Media and MP3 to offer outstanding quality even at high compression. Again, you can download a free encoder (http://www.microsoft.com/windows/windowsmedia/default.aspx) or use the encoding tools in your audio software.

▶ **MP3.** This popular format was actually developed for the audio portion of the DVD video format. Even at high compression rates, the files sound very good and are much smaller than regular CD-quality .wav files. This is why it became the most popular format on the Web. It's an ideal format for your online demo and for sending auditions to agencies and even finished files to certain clients. Most audio software encodes to MP3, or you can surf the Net for other shareware or freeware encoders. Type "MP3 encoder" in Google for some ideas.

Streaming versus Download

There are two ways to access sound files on the Internet—streaming or download. When a file streams, it plays in real time. The audio player, such as Window Media Player, buffers a little of the file first, which essentially means that it loads the first part of the audio file into memory. Then the file starts and the player grabs the rest of the file in the background. Depending on the file, the encoder used, and the Internet connection, you can hear the file play with few or no interruptions. Typical streaming files include Real Media and Windows Media files.

When you download a sound file, you must save the entire file to your hard drive before you can start playing it, such as with an MP3 (although you can stream them, too).

Preparing Your Files for Encoding

After you've cleaned up, edited, and polished your performance, save the file as an uncompressed CD-quality file. This is your master file. From it you could burn a high-quality CD to send out. However, this file is not yet ready for the Web. Instead, you need to treat it before you encode it. Why? Follow these tips and your files will simply sound better.

Open the master file in your audio editor (in this example, the Sound Forge editor). Use EQ to carefully shape the sound you will encode. EQ was, as you no doubt remember, ET's younger and much better-looking brother. He was, however, quite diminutive—short, in our parlance—though. EQ in the audio world is similarly short—short for the term *equalization*. EQ, the audio kind, lets you affect the tonal qualities of a sound file. You can emphasize certain frequencies, such as bringing out more highs or eliminating some low-end rumble. To prepare your file for the Web, roll off everything below 100 Hz and above 10,000 Hz (10 kHz) rather sharply. Not all of the compression encoders respond well to extremely low- or high-frequency content. This EQ trick eliminates these frequencies, leaving a sound file that sounds better after final encoding.

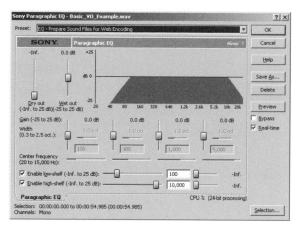

Use equalization (EQ) to prepare your files for Web encoding.

After processing the file with EQ, consider reducing its dynamic range. The difference between the loudest and the softest parts of a sound file comprises its dynamic range. For MP3 and other Web encoding, it's best to *limit* that dynamic range to about 12 dB. This means you need to squeeze a larger amount of sound energy down a smaller pipe. Compression is the primary way to squeeze those dynamics; it's the funnel you use to do this. By decreasing the volume of louder sounds and moving them closer to softer sounds, the compressor works to level the overall volume. See Chapter 8, "Advanced Techniques," for details.

For voice tracks, set the threshold level about three to six decibels below the loudest peak level. In other words, if your loudest peak in your recording is at −3 dB on the digital meters, set your threshold at about −9 dB. Try a 4:1 ratio. Set the attack medium fast, about 20 ms, and the release to a long setting, about 500 ms. This setting will smooth out your recording by only compressing the loudest sounds. If you feel you still need a little more compression, experiment with the threshold and ratio settings.

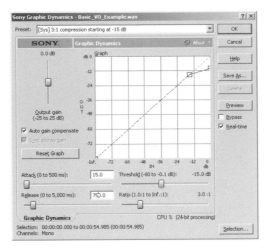

Use compression to squeeze the dynamic range of your sound file, too.

With your file EQed and compressed, you need to maximize its overall level through a process called *normalization*. Essentially, normalization increases the overall volume of a sound file. You have two choices—peak and RMS. With *peak normalizing*, you set a maximum volume level. The software then takes the loudest peak in your sound file and moves it to the level you picked. The software also increases the level of the rest of the waveform by the same amount it boosted the peak. If you set the peak normalization to –1 dB and the current highest peak level is –6 dB, the software will boost the volume five decibels for the whole file.

RMS normalizing increases the average volume of the file, what might be called *perceived loudness*. Normalizing using RMS settings is often unpredictable for the novice. RMS is based on the average level, which is far lower than the peak level, and frankly, it is just far too hard to explain without Harlan falling asleep. Long story short: Stick to peak normalization.

Using the normalization tools provided by your audio software, peak normalize to –0.10 dB. For the Sound Forge application, this would also be 98.86 percent. That's plenty loud for Internet compression encoding.

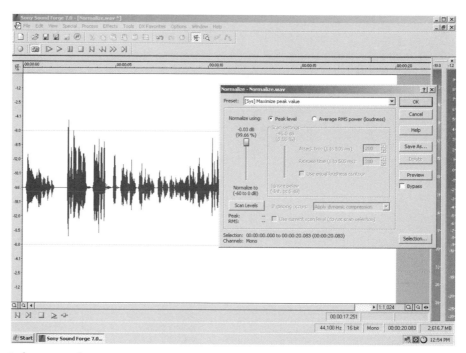

Before normalization

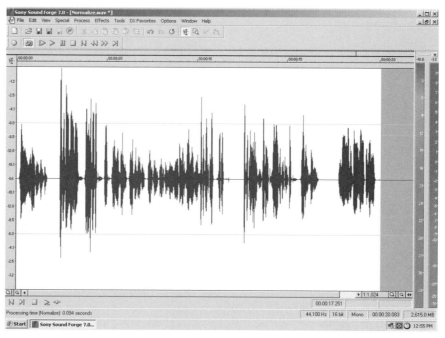

Normalization helps maximize the volume of your sound file. Note the difference in the amplitude (volume) between the before and after examples.

Now your file is ready to encode to Real Media, Windows Media, and/or MP3. We suggest that you save this file first to uncompressed CD-quality and give it a different name than your master file. Perhaps add "web" to the file name to help you remember which file is which. Then, use this alternate Web-ready file to create your encoded files.

Choose the 128 Kbps setting when compressing larger audio files to MP3.

The Sony Media Software Wave Hammer Plug-In

The full-blown Pro version of the Sound Forge software includes a special Wave Hammer plug-in. As its name implies, the Wave Hammer plug-in helps you maximize the volume of your sound files through a combination of compression and normalization. The software automatically applies some gentle compression to your sound file, and then maximizes that output to a setting you indicate.

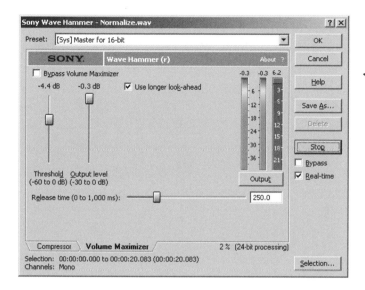

This tool is ideal for preparing your files for Web encoding. First, apply the EQ as indicated in the text, and then use the Wave Hammer tool to apply final compression and normalization in one operation.

For the compression settings, set the threshold to −10 dB, the ratio to 4.5:1, the output gain to −0.3 dB (that's *point* three dB). Also, check the Peak Scan Mode radio button and the Auto Gain Compensate check box. For the Volume Maximizer setting, choose −0.1 dB (again, that's *point* one). The result will be a loud, in-your-face sound perfect for preparing the file prior to Web encoding.

Virtual Voiceover

Many of us started out to be actors, treading the boards to the appreciative applause of theatergoers. Soon, we found ourselves waiting tables, even when we had successful theatrical careers. So we discovered voiceover work as a way to pay the bills and use our acting talent in what the business folks call a *niche market*. Others of us started in broadcasting, and as station after station was gobbled up by corporate America, found ourselves in a dying profession dominated by only a handful of performers. We, too, looked to voiceover work as a way of using our skills and paying the bills.

Now actor and broadcaster alike have to—re-read that—*have to* embrace the reality that the voiceover business has also changed. Just as we don't frequently run down to the local stationery supply store or local bookstore anymore, our clients don't simply call a local talent agent and say, "Book 'em."

This is a virtual world, and we can be part of it by welcoming new technology and getting ourselves—actually, our voices—up into cyberspace for a waiting and appreciative audience. Or we can sit back and reminisce about the way it used to be. You make the call, but the smart money's on becoming a virtual voiceover.

Video	Audio
	Narrator:
B-Roll: Modern family sitting in the living room in the glow of computers; mom surfing the Web on a wireless laptop; dad reading an e-book on a 20" flat screen monitor; the children playing with a Sony PlayStation	**...there's** no doubt that things will never be quite the same again.

8 } Advanced Techniques

Capturing a solid performance into your computer with a good volume level and lack of noise will probably be all you need for most of your work. However, there are some advanced techniques that can take your voice recordings to a higher level. We divide these techniques into two categories—fixing and sweetening. *Fixing* involves using the tools to hide mistakes and repair other errors. *Sweetening* is using tricks to make your voice recordings extraordinary. These tricks can range from compression, EQ, and reverb to adding music and sound effects to your finished pieces.

Got This Problem?

Common errors such as blown lines, lip smacks, extraneous noises, and other gremlins require your attention when editing. Deleting the unwanted parts and rearranging the best sections is straightforward once you get the hang of it. Here are some other common problems and how to fix them.

Some of these fixes are only marginally effective. Try to get good, clean sounds recorded in the first place so you won't have to resort to these tricks.

Lip Smacks

Have you ever really listened to a kiss? The sound is positively gross close up, particularly if you are receiving the kiss-off or the kiss of death or if some French person wipes out both of your ears with that weird air-kiss thing they do. Our brains are actually pretty adept at ignoring unpleasant sounds, but recordings have a way of magnifying and amplifying sounds that might not even register with us in real life, and nothing sounds more unprofessional than an annoying "tick" every time you open your mouth. You usually hear these lip smacks at sentence starts and occasionally on certain words. Reduce them as well as other mouth noises at the source. Keep your mouth and throat lubricated. Avoid cold and hot liquids. Instead, have some room-temperature water nearby when recording. Also, moisten those lips with some saliva—or better still and less disgusting, lip balm.

If a lip smack or two slips through, eliminate them using your audio editing software. They usually stick out as a small bump in the waveform just before a word begins. If you can't see a lip smack but you can hear it, try zooming in for a closer look. Find the smack, select it, and either mute or simply delete it.

Shall I mute or delete, that is the question. When you select a sound wave or a portion thereof and mute it, the sound volume is reduced to nothing—in other words, silence. When you delete a portion, the section is removed completely. Obviously, this also affects the length of the take. So if you need the time of your performance to remain the same, but you want to eliminate something, use mute. If the timing can change, use delete.

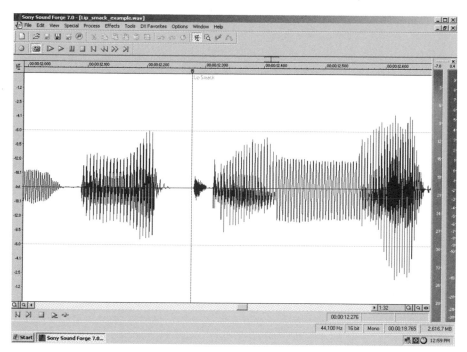

Notice the little waveform just before the bigger one? That's a lip smack that begs to be cut out. Select it and delete it. Please.

Another nauseating noise that can slip into recordings comes from dentures. Make sure they're firmly in place before a session. You don't want them clicking around during a take.

Breaths
Gasps at the beginning of sentences are the worst. We already talked about this in Chapter 4. Again, eliminate bad breathing while recording or resort to cutting it out later. Alternatively, you might be able to use a noise gate to automatically eliminate some breathing sounds. See the "General Background Noise" section later in this chapter.

Extraneous Noise
"To be…[beep beep]…or not…[honk]…to be…[screeeeeeeech]…that is the…[CRASH!]…." If this is your typical session, you might want to consider recording someplace else. Work to get the most noise-free recording you can. It will make your life so much easier. Occasionally, even in professional studios with thousands of dollars of soundproofing, an unwanted sound will creep in. If you hear it when recording, simply redo the line. Unfortunately, sometimes you're so focused on delivery that you don't notice the noise until playback. Again, you're better off re-recording the messed up section rather than trying to salvage the take. If that's not possible, try

editing the take. If the noise falls between words or phrases, simply remove it. However, if the noise competes with your speaking, you'll need to try some other tricks. Other sound elements, such as music, can help mask or cover up extraneous noises, but that's not the best solution either.

Equalization (EQ, for short) lets you control the tonal characteristics of a sound. Think treble and bass on your home or car stereo, and you'll understand EQ basics. Turn up the bass and make the music go thump, thump, thump. This is especially useful for annoying crabby neighbors. Turn up the treble and the recording will sound bright to the point of being brittle and shrill—great for freaking out the crabby neighbor's mangy cat and snarling dog. Audio editing software gives you greater control than simply adjusting treble and bass, though. You can really zero in on the audio frequency of trouble spots and boost or reduce them until the recording sounds better. Try using EQ to cut offending frequencies rather than boosting in other areas. For example, to make a recording sound brighter, try reducing the middle range a little instead of boosting the treble. Also, EQ changes the volume of your sound file—so be careful the level doesn't get too loud and clip!

For extraneous noises, listen carefully to the sound. Is it a low sound, such as a thump? Or is it a high sound, such as a squeaky chair? If it falls in the middle, EQ will be less effective because your voice is in those middle frequencies, too. In your audio editing software, highlight the part of your recording where the noise resides. Use EQ to reduce its impact. It will take some trial and error before you find the right setting. Let your ears help you judge whether the sound gets better, worse, or stays the same as you adjust the settings. In some cases, EQ won't work at all and you'll have to live with the noise.

Hotels, where you might be doing a quick audition to e-mail to your agent, always seem to put voice actors in the rooms closest to the vending machines, ice machines, and elevator. There's nothing like the whoosh of the elevator doors or the bang of a soda can dropping to ruin a perfectly good track. Believe us, it's much easier to just re-record than to try to "fix it in the mix," as the pros say.

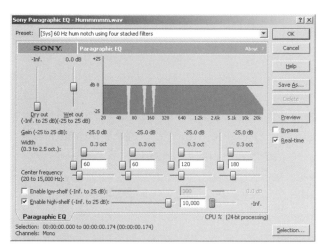

EQ, or equalization, lets you adjust the tonal characteristics of a sound file.

General Background Noise

Instead of a single distinct noise in your recording, you might have an overall noisy din. Air conditioners, computer fans, distant traffic—all these can add an unwanted sound element that you should eliminate. You might also want to remove some breaths, paper rustling, or other low-volume sounds automatically, instead of manually hunting them down and deleting them.

A noise gate is one effective way to dump the noise. As its name implies, the noise gate lets the good sounds through when it is open, and it shuts out hiss and other background anomalies when it is closed. Noise gates typically have three settings—threshold, attack, and release. It's pretty much what the warden tells new prisoners: "During your incarceration, should your behavior cross over my pre-determined *threshold* of acceptability, you'll get *attacked* by a large number of burly guards and trustees, but if you stay calm and polite, before long you'll get *released* with a new suit and twenty bucks in your pocket. Do I make myself clear?"

Threshold adjusts how strong a signal must be before the gate (picture a cell door swinging wide) will open. When the signal falls below the threshold setting, the gate closes. *Attack* determines how fast the gate will open once the signal reaches above the threshold. *Release* determines how long it will take for the gate to close after the signal falls below the threshold. Short times chop off the sound, while longer times offer smoother decays.

Noise gate thresholds are easy to set. Start with the gate fully open (infinity) and play the file. Slowly increase the threshold until you continue to hear your voice but the noise disappears between phrases. Be careful not to accidentally chop off the starts and ends of words; lower the threshold a little if this happens. Always listen to your entire recording after applying the noise gate to be extra sure you didn't chop off something. If you did, undo the noise gate, readjust the settings, and try again. And a gentle reminder one mo' time: If you have taken our advice and made copies of the original file, you'll always be able to undo any damage you may have done! The downside of noise gates is that they only shut out noise when no other sound is present. The noise will continue under your speaking parts, but your voice should mask it. Unfortunately, you might hear the noise gate working. The background noise will appear under your talking, and then disappear when you pause. This situation often makes a noisy recording sound even worse. People will hear the "jumps" of noise and silence, ruining the impression you are trying to convey. Either adjust the noise gate controls until the recording sounds smoother or scrap the idea entirely.

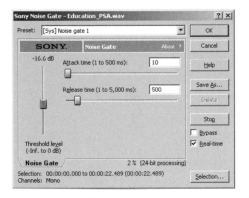

A noise gate will eliminate noise between words and phrases.

Ironically, our ears/brain combination is more adept at tuning out constant noise than noise that disappears and reappears regularly. Therefore, leaving the noise in, if it's constant and not totally distracting, might be the best solution.

Noise reduction is another fix-it tool that can salvage some recordings. Sony Media Software makes a powerful little utility that works wonders on background noise. The program is a DirectX plug-in, which just means it needs a host program to work properly; it doesn't run on its own. You can only use it with the full-blown professional version of the Sound Forge application. Audition and several other audio software programs include their own noise reduction utilities. Noise reduction works by analyzing the waveform and then separating the noise from the good stuff. The program then applies its filters in real time to eliminate the noise. Unlike a noise gate, the software even eliminates the noise while you're speaking. While we suggest you work to get noise-free recordings by building an isolation booth, locating your studio carefully, and recording loud levels well above the noise, this tool can save you in a pinch.

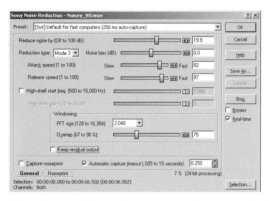

This utility can help make noisy recordings sound cleaner.

Hum and Hiss

We're not sure which is worse, the annoying zzzzz of a 60-Hz electrical hum or the equally irksome sssss of hiss. Both are byproducts of electronic gear that you should do your best to avoid. Eliminate hum by keeping your cables as short as possible and keeping electrical cords far away from mic cables. If a mic cable must cross an electrical cable, do so at right angles (90 degrees). Keep the mic away from the computer monitor, too, because that can introduce noise into your recording.

Hum is often caused by ground loops, which are essentially multiple paths to ground for electricity. The fix is usually one of those three-prong to two-prong adapters (called a *ground lift*) used on the electrical cord of the humming appliance. Computers and monitors have grounded plugs, but some mixers and audio interface devices do not. Use the ground lift on your mixer/audio interface to see whether the hum will go away. Hey, for less than 50 cents, it's worth a try.

Hiss comes from some cheap gear (preamps, mixers) or when volume settings are turned up too high. For example, you might have the faders on your mixer maxed out, introducing hiss. What you really need to do is lower their level and get more gain from the microphone preamp instead. Proper gain staging, as discussed *ad nauseum* in Chapter 4, is vital to making noise-free recordings.

EQ is another way to eliminate hum and hiss. As a rule, use EQ to greatly reduce all frequencies below 100 Hz. There's very little voice information that low, but there is a lot of low-end junk, rumble, and hum. Engage the EQ roll off switch on your mic before you record, if it has one. Alternatively, use EQ at your mixer to roll off the lows. Or, when editing, after running the DC offset, use EQ to roll off all the frequencies below 100 Hz on every voice recording. Roll off everything above 12 kHz to contain hiss. Cutting hiss is best left to do while editing, when you can make sure that reducing this frequency range doesn't make your recording sound too dull.

High pass, low pass, and do not pass Go! Sometimes EQ settings are referred to as **high-pass** *or* **low-pass** *filters. As the name implies, a high-pass filter lets the high frequencies, or treble, through while cutting out the low bass frequencies. A low-pass filter lets the bass through, cutting out the high frequencies in the process. Many professional mics have a high-pass switch that effectively cuts out the extreme low frequencies. We suggest you engage that switch if your mic offers it. It won't hurt the quality of your voice, but it will improve the quality of your recordings by keeping low bass frequencies (some of which you may not even hear) out of them.*

Bad Edits

Always run the DC Offset utility before you make any change to a sound file. This ensures that the center line or zero crossing is correctly aligned. Refer back to Chapter 4 for details about DC offset. Make sure when you edit the file, you cut where the sound wave crosses that center line, too. Otherwise, you might introduce a pop or click into the recording. Also, be careful not to accidentally cut off the starts and ends of words. Listen back to *every* edit before continuing.

One simple little trick that can really smooth over bad edits is to apply a quick fade to them. Highlight from the start of the offending section over to the right a tiny amount, say a quarter of a second or less. Apply a quick fade-in if the section is at the start of a word or a fade-out if the section is at the end. Practice this technique until you feel really comfortable with it, because it can really disguise bad edits and other anomalies.

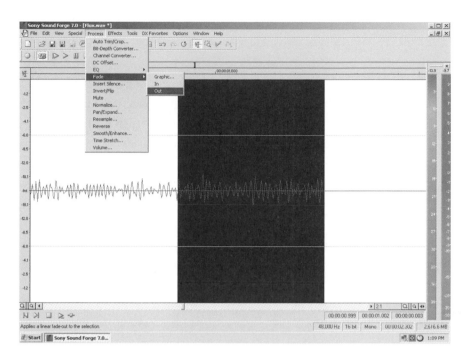

Quick fades (in or out) can disguise bad edits and other unwanted sounds.

Sentence Pickups

So you made a mistake. Should you just pick it up from there and move on? No! No! No! Never record sentence pickups where you only redo part of a line. No matter how expertly you edit the mistake, we guarantee the sentence pickup will not match the surrounding words. The emotion and delivery will be all wrong, making the sentence fragment stick out like a sore thumb. Always return to the sentence start (and sometimes even further back than that) when you re-record the take. Your delivery will sound smoother and more natural, and you'll reduce your editing chores considerably.

Volume Inconsistencies

Several factors can make some parts of your recorded file sound louder than other parts. Your delivery might be inconsistent. You might have turned away from the mic slightly. Or there could be any number of performance issues. You also might have set your initial recording levels too low or too high. Thankfully, there are several ways to even out the volume levels.

The simplest method is to find the parts that are too loud and decrease their volume. Simply select the loud section, choose the volume tool in your software, and reduce the volume by a few decibels. Tweak the amount until it sounds right. Comparing the section you're fixing to the nearby waveforms can visually show whether your levels are consistent. A loud peak is easy to spot onscreen. Listen to the surrounding words and make sure the level change sounds natural, too. You can try the same trick on soft sections, increasing the volume a few decibels at a time until it works with the whole file. In digital audio, a 6-dB swing means the sound will be four times as loud or as soft—and that's a *big* change. Start with small adjustments and go from there.

Compression lets you even the volume, too. This tool squeezes the *dynamic range* (the difference between the loudest and the softest passages). A compressor acts as a funnel that decreases the volume of louder sounds, moving them closer to the softer sounds. The overall dynamic range is smaller, and the volume is more even. Then, you can boost the level of the whole track after you compress it, making it sound louder overall.

How does a compressor work? It has several interactive sections.

THRESHOLD
When the recording exceeds a specific threshold level set by the controls, the compressor kicks in by reducing that level depending on the ratio setting. (See the following section.) Any signal below the threshold setting is unaffected, while all signals above the threshold are "squeezed," or compressed.

RATIO
Ratio settings determine how the output is compressed. Ratios can be set at unity (1:1) up to infinity to one. In other words, at a 1:1 ratio, a 1-dB signal change results in a 1-dB output (no gain or unity gain). At other ratios, the output is reduced by relative amounts. At 4:1, a 4-dB increase in input level results in only a 1-dB output level gain. That's the powerful squeezing function of the compressor that is so useful for leveling the volume of your recordings.

ATTACK
Attack sets the time it takes before a recording above the threshold starts being compressed. This important setting ensures that quick transients—fast, almost percussive sounds, such as many hard consonants—remain unaffected before the compression grabs on to the sound. Low settings squeeze signals fast and hard, while higher settings let the punch of the consonants through. If the setting is too low, certain words might sound chopped off. You'll hear a sort of sucking sound, as if the volume was pulled

down really fast (which is what is really happening). If the setting is too high, loud passages might go through without the compressor having a chance to squeeze them, defeating the whole purpose of using the compressor.

RELEASE

Release is like attack, only in reverse. This control determines how long it takes for the compressor to return to unity gain (its original volume level) after the signal has dropped below the threshold. Again, you can vary the time from very short to very long. Short times act on the signal, constantly producing some unnatural staccato effects, while long times are smooth and more forgiving.

OUTPUT

The output control helps you add volume back into the signal that is often lost during the other processing steps. This extra gain is what makes the compressed file sound louder.

Most audio editors include compression of some kind, and a little goes a long way! Try a threshold that's just a few decibels below the loudest peak level in your file. For the ratio setting, start with 1.5:1 and consider increasing that to 4:1 if it still sounds good. Keep the attack medium fast, about 15–25 milliseconds, and the release long, more than a second.

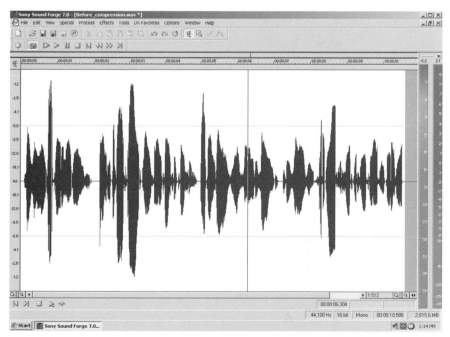

Compressors reduce the dynamic range of your recordings, leveling the overall volume. Notice the peaks in the before example in relation to the softer sounds.

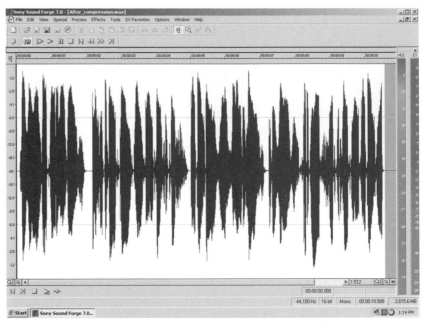

Check out the more even and louder overall level in this example.

Clicks

There are several sources for clicks in your recordings in addition to the lip smacks and mouth noises we talked about earlier. Mics and digital errors can also make clicking sounds. Microphones can sometimes pop or click if too much moisture gets on the diaphragm. This moisture can come from an overly humid room or from you! Always use a pop filter to keep your spittle where it should be—on you, not on your microphone. Digital errors can sometimes occur in your software program, and you might hear little digital ticks or clicks in your recording. These sounds will appear as spikes, which can be easily seen and quickly edited in your audio editor. However, if the problem is a recurring one, it's likely that you haven't set up the program correctly to play well with your soundcard and/or A-to-D converter. Re-read the manual or call the software provider for help. Usually it's a fairly simple matter of adjusting where files are stored in the computer or changing the size of buffers used by your software.

Thin Sound

For a male voice, use EQ to add about 2 to 4 dB at 160 Hz. This frequency range boosts the natural deep resonance of the male voice, giving depth and authority to it. For a female voice, thicken up the sound by adding 2 to 4 dB at 320 Hz.

Dull Recording

Use EQ to add 2 to 4 dB between 10 and 12 kHz. Cut 2 to 4 dB at 700 Hz, what Jeffrey affectionately calls the "mud zone." Avoid the 4- to 7-kHz range because that's where sibilance resides. Boosting levels here can make S sounds harsh and distorted, though. Let your ears judge whether the fix is better than the original. Often things sound *different*, but not better.

Louder File

Make sure your levels are reasonably high. You want to get as close to digital zero as possible without exceeding it! As we mentioned in Chapter 4, digital zero is a brick wall. Digital recording can't and won't handle any volume above zero; it simply clips off the waveform (and you hear distortion—ugly, nasty distortion). Digital zero is different from the analog world's 0VU, where exceeding it was okay. Because the meters in your software recording application use digital zero, don't go there or above it.

Despite your best attempts, you might still feel your levels are low. You can increase the overall level in three ways—using normalization, compression, or loudness maximizers. Be aware that boosting the level of quiet sounds can bring up more noise, too. All that ugliness masked by your thunderous performance starts to share the spotlight when you increase the level of quiet passages.

When you normalize a digital file, you increase the overall volume to a level you decide. The software looks for the loudest peak in the recording and increases its volume to match the setting you chose. It also boosts the rest of the file by the same amount, maintaining the file's original volume relationships. The effect makes the overall file sound louder. However, if you have one huge peak in a file and the rest is low in level, the boost may be negligible. Instead, exclude that one loud peak when you apply normalization, and let the software work on the remainder of the file.

Apply compression to squeeze the dynamic range, and the perceived overall volume will be louder. Review the "Volume Inconsistencies" section earlier in the chapter for more information. A special kind of compressor, called a *volume maximizer*, can make your file sound really loud. The Sound Forge software includes a Wave Hammer utility that can slam your sound files close to digital zero without clipping. (See Chapter 7's discussion on encoding for details.)

Another form of compression—what you might call *extreme compression*—is known as *limiting*. Remember the ratio setting we mentioned in our discussion about compressors? When the ratio starts to get too high, say 10:1 and above, the compressor turns into a limiter. With a limiter, no matter how loud your recording is, the output volume is kept at a constant level. Heavy limiting can squeeze the life out of a performance by making the softest parts as loud as the loudest sections. The volume is the same throughout the performance. Use this feature with care, or your recordings might sound very loud and in-your-face, but lack any subtlety.

Harlan loves to apply a little compression and normalization to his auditions. They make his voice sound louder than the voices of the other actors vying for the part. It's the kind of simple trick that can make your work stand out from the crowd.

Faster/Slower

You can control time with some software tools. Voice track running a little long? Time compress it. Too fast? Spread it out. Time compression works by speeding up the file based on the settings you choose. Of course, speeding it up means you'll start to sound like a Munchkin from the *Wizard of Oz*, right? Wrong. The software simultaneously shifts the pitch down to the original frequency. You talk faster at the same pitch. Time expansion slows the file down and shifts the pitch up, also maintaining the original voice quality, only slower. These effects are only marginally effective. After about a 10-percent change either way, the quality suffers. An odd metallic, swishy sound, called *phasing*, happens with time compression. And time expansion sounds like...well, like you're stoned. That is, if we knew what stoned people sounded like (but we don't).

A better tactic for speeding up or slowing down involves a little editing. To save time, carefully remove pauses from between phrases and even words. By tightening up the performance, you often can make a track shorter, and it still sounds natural. You'll be surprised how cutting tiny amounts really adds up to significant timing changes without hurting the performance. If you need to slow your take down, simply add silence in at appropriate times to lengthen the track.

Plosives

Use microphone techniques to eliminate popped Ps and Ts while recording. Try miking from the side and/or using a pop filter. Work on your voice to control those plosives, too. When editing, a little special compression can work; see the following "Sibilance" section.

Sibilance

Once again, microphone technique (try side miking) and choice of microphone are your first choices in the battle to overcome sizzling esses. When editing, apply a little EQ to reduce minor sibilance. Try removing 2 to 4 dB between 5 and 8 kHz. That's where those esses hide out. You might need to adjust this somewhat lower for an alto and higher for a soprano. Another nice tool is a de-esser. This special software combines a multiband compressor and EQ. Basically, the compressor kicks in *only* when the sibilant frequencies (or loud plosives) are present, reducing them significantly. When there's no sibilance present, the de-esser lays low and doesn't affect the sound. This same technique can reduce plosives somewhat, too. The Sound Forge software and other applications include some preset settings for reducing plosives and sibilance effectively.

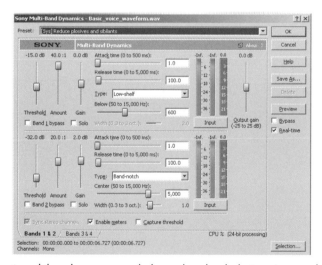

A multiband compressor helps reduce loud plosives (popped Ps and Bs) and control sibilance (excessive S sounds).

Clipping

If you've broken the big no-no and let your recordings exceed the dreaded digital zero, they will sound distorted—or clipped. Although you can reduce the volume of a clipped waveform to under zero, it will still sound distorted. Aside from re-recording the clipped part, there's very little you can do. The noise reduction plug-in mentioned earlier includes a clip restoration utility that might help with quick clips, but not with large sections. Audition also has several clip restoration features that might save you…or not. So don't record past digital zero! Ever. Got it? You sure? Well, okay then. Let's move on.

Adding Some Pizzazz

Most of your sound editing will entail fixing mistakes. But once in a while you get to expand your horizons and move into more creative areas. While there's any number of creative effects you can apply, the following sections list some of the most useful ones.

Telephone Sound

Use a graphic EQ to boost 1 kHz a little, and then cut all the other frequency bands around it. You'll be left with that telltale telephone sound.

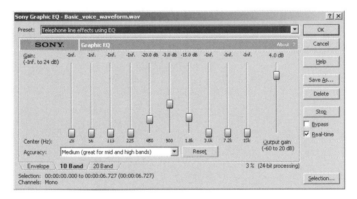

Make your voice sound like it was recorded over a telephone with this EQ trick.

Caverns and Hallways and Bathrooms, Oh My

Large spaces and small, live rooms have distinctive sounds that are easy to recreate in software. *Reverberation* (reverb, for short) is a byproduct of sound bouncing around a room. It's actually a series of closely spaced echoes that blend to form a room sound. Clap your hands sharply in a parking garage to hear reverb in action. Software reverbs use sophisticated mathematical algorithms to recreate the sound of spaces. Forget about it! Just choose a setting that sounds good to your ears. Often the descriptions of the settings provide a clue, such as Cathedral, Small Hall, and so forth. Beware of really long reverbs because things might start to sound a little mushy. A little goes a long way. Also, if you need to add reverb to your voice, make sure it's one of the last things you do after you've finished editing. Otherwise, you'll have a hard time matching up edits.

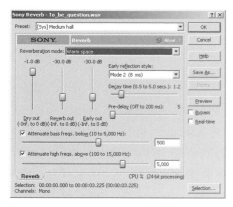

Put your voice in a variety of different spaces using reverb.

Echoes

Applying distinct repeats to your voice gives the echo sound you might need. You use a delay to accomplish this. The delay repeats whatever you send to it after a specified amount of time has elapsed. The settings determine how long before the delay starts, how many delays there will be, and how long it will take for the delay to die away. A single repeat will sound like the echo in the mountains. Multiple repeats sound a little different. By feeding a little of the delayed sound back into the delay again, more echoes come out. The result is that twittering echo sound of John Lennon's vocals on the Beatles' "A Day in the Life."

Swirlies

No, we're not talking about shoving somebody's head in a toilet bowl and flushing. Might be a fulfilling fantasy exercised on some of the morons we've worked with, though. Stress relief aside, there are several effects that impart a dreamy, swirly effect on your voice. Flanging, chorusing, and phasing are the solution. Some audio editors include these effects; rather than waste valuable space trying to explain them, you'd be better served by taking a sample file and applying these effects to them and listening. Like what you hear? Remember what you did and use it when it makes sense.

Pitch Shifting

Turning males into females and vice versa is the realm of the pitch shifter (and some surgeons in Sweden). Although obvious Chipmunks and Darth Vader extremes are possible, many subtle effects can be realized, too. Pitch-shift software is often musically-based, so you'll see references to musical intervals (thirds, octaves, and so on). Just play around until you find what you're listening for.

Take the sound of a baby crying and shift its pitch down one octave, and you'll get the unmistakable sound of a teenager whining. If anyone ever asks you what the difference is between a baby and a teenager, tell 'em one octave.

Not long ago Harlan produced a public service announcement in his home studio, and even though the voice performer he'd booked was a senior citizen and turned in a wonderful performance, Harlan's clients in New York felt he sounded too young when they heard the finished recording. Rather than re-record (and pay) another performer, Harlan tweaked the same reading with the pitch controls in Adobe Audition and voila—his clients unanimously approved and applauded the "new," "older" actor!

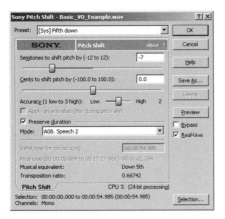

Change your voice into a chipmunk's or Darth Vader's using a pitch shift effect.

Adding Music and Sound Effects

While the majority of your work will remain strictly voice, there might be times when you require additional production elements, namely music and sound effects.

Sound Effects

There are three kinds of sound effects. *Hard effects* correspond to the action in the scene, such as a door slam when a character exits. *Soft effects* don't underscore any action; instead, they serve to reinforce a scene's reality. A soft effect might be a car horn for a scene on a busy city street. *Ambient sound effects*, or *backgrounds*, provide a general overall soundscape, such as playground sounds at a park.

You can buy sound effects as library CDs and online. Several companies release CDs jam-packed with almost any sound you can imagine. If you will be heavy into this kind of production, investing in a few quality libraries is a sound idea, so to speak. On the other hand, if you only need an occasional effect from time to time, consider purchasing effects on the Web as needed. The fee usually runs around $15.00 per effect. Remember that by paying the fee to the sound effect owner for a CD library or a downloaded sound, you can legally use it in your productions. If you steal an effect, you might be hearing the sound of the prison door slamming or at least a bank account emptying to pay for your legal defense! Check out these sound effects sources:

▶ The Hollywood Edge (http://www.hollywoodedge.com)

▶ Sonomic (http://www.sonomic.com)

▶ SoundDogs.com (http://www.sounddogs.com)

▶ Sound-Effects-Library.com (http://www.sound-effects-library.com)

▶ Sound Ideas of America (http://www.soundideas.com)

You also can create your own sound effects. Bring props into your studio and record what you need right there. Or grab a very long microphone cable or even a portable recorder, such as a Mini Disc recorder, and have fun capturing the sounds of your world. As an alternative, use your mouth to emulate the effects you need. Mouth sounds are great for cartoon effects and even a few dramatic ones, too. Later, you can use your audio software to manipulate these sounds further, at the same time stretching your creativity and budget.

Music
There are two ways to use music—source and underscore. *Source music* emanates from within the scene, such as music coming from a radio. *Underscore* is the dramatic music needed to accent the drama.

Where do you get the music you need? You might think you could grab a CD off the shelf and drop in a track or two from your favorite artist. Unfortunately, using copyrighted material is a big no-no, as we just pointed out. You can hire a composer, but that might cost more than your budget allows.

You can buy library music specifically created and licensed for A/V use, just as you would sound effects. Buyout licenses are cost effective because you pay only one fee, and then you can use the music non-exclusively whenever you want. Sources for music libraries include:

▶ FirstCom Music (http://www.firstcom.com)

▶ Fresh Music (http://www.freshmusic.com)

▶ Killer Tracks (http://www.killertracks.com)

▶ Melomania (http://www.jeffreypfisher.com/melo.html)

▶ Music Bakery (http://www.musicbakery.com)

▶ Omnimusic (http://www.omnimusic.com)

▶ VideoHelper (http://www.videohelper.com)

And, you can compose your own music. Huh? We can hear you saying, "I'm no musician. I can't write my own music." Guess what? You *can* compose your own music with a little help from technology.

ACID software is a powerful and popular Windows program from Sony Media Software that helps you create music scores quickly. It's both easy to learn and fun to use. No musical skill is required, either. The ACID application essentially lets you choose and combine music and sound "loops" to create your own original, royalty-free music. It's a snap to pick sounds, paint them on a grid, and make music. Adobe Audition handles loops as well. GarageBand, part of Apple's iLife suite, is another fun way to make your own music.

And what are loops? A music loop is a pre-recorded, usually short snippet of a musical performance that repeats flawlessly and (if you want) continuously, hence the term "loops." Loops come as CD-quality sound files, usually in .wav format. A single loop might be a drum beat, a bass guitar riff, a piano part, or something else. By selecting and arranging different musical loops, you create new songs. Purchased loops are royalty-free, and the finished compositions you create from them belong to you.

The retail version of the ACID software includes a content CD with hundreds of loops to get you started. Adobe Audition (http://www.adobe.com) includes more than 5,000 downloadable loops free with its software. GarageBand is similarly decked out. Best of all, you can choose from a huge inventory of other music loops in a variety of styles—rock, orchestral, hip-hop, techno, ethnic/world, electronica, ambient, and nearly everything in between and out on the extreme fringe. You can get additional loop libraries from Sony Media Software and other vendors, such as Big Fish Audio (http://www.bigfishaudio.com), Masterbits (http://www.masterbits.de), Q Up Arts (http://www.quparts.com), and Sonomic (http://www.sonomic.com).

If you think this might be a fun, creative way to enhance your voice productions, grab the ACID Xpress software *free* from ACIDplanet.com (http://www.acidplanet.com). This version is limited to playing only 10-tracks of loops, but it otherwise functions the same as the rest of the product line. Also, each week you can download a sample composition and eight free loops, called *8 packs*, at ACIDplanet.com. This way you can learn and hear how other people use the program. Then you can create your compositions with the free loops you download.

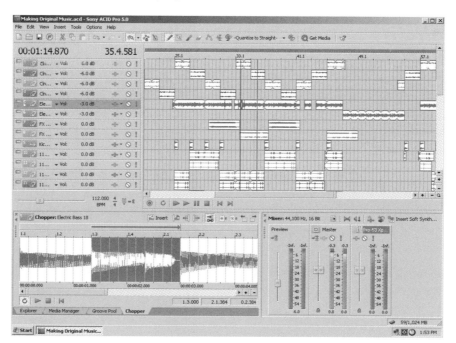

Programs such as the ACID application make it easy to create your own royalty-free music scores.

Mixing in Music and Sound Effects

Adding sound effects and music to your voice work with your audio software is an easy affair. After completing the finished voice track, select the sound effects and music you need and get them on your hard drive. How you add them to your recordings might vary depending on the audio editing software you use.

In the Sound Forge software, open the sound effect you need to insert in a separate window, select it, and copy it to the clipboard. Switch to your finished voice track and position the cursor where you want to add the effect. Hit Paste to add the sound effect. To add music or sound effects that occur along with the voice track, use Paste Special > Mix. This method lets you adjust the volume of the effect or music in relation to the original voice. It's not the easiest way to work, though. If you are going to do a lot of production work like this, invest in multitrack audio software to make your audio work easier and better.

Extracting Audio from CD

Sometimes the sound effects or music you need is on audio CDs. Both the Sound Forge and Audition applications include a handy utility for extracting tracks. In the Sound Forge application go to File > Extract Audio from CD, select the track in the dialog box, choose a name and location for the .wav file, and then let the Sound Forge application do the work for you. With the music or sound effect in .wav format, you can add it to your project easily.

Multitracking

So far we've talked mostly about using a stereo or mono audio recording and editing program for the majority of your work. There is another class of audio software that you should know about. *Multitrack audio software*, as its name implies, lets you keep different audio tracks (voice, sound effects, and music) separate and then mix them later. Multitracking allows you to play several different character parts in a scene or simply talk to and answer yourself. Best of all, multitrack software gives you greater creative control over your final projects. Just right for control freaks like us!

Multitracking is the mainstay of music recording. All the parts that comprise a popular song are kept separate from the other parts. Sometimes the musicians play together; other times they don't. Vocals, in particular, are almost always added after the basic background track is recorded.

Keeping the elements separate gives the producer better control over the finished recording.

Think of a collage, and this whole concept might make better sense to you. Picture the individual sounds as bits of paper and the multitrack software as the canvas and glue that hold them all together.

How does that apply to you? Think of a fictional radio commercial. Scene: Busy supermarket. Three voices: Husband, wife, and narrator. Using multitrack software, you record the husband on one track, the wife on another, and the narrator on a third. Using a sound effects CD, you add a supermarket background loop to a fourth track. And finally, you select some music to help deliver the message and put it on the fifth track.

With this configuration you can control the relative volume of all the sound elements. The supermarket background sound could start out loud, and then get softer when the actors speak. The music could start in the middle of the scene when the narrator adds his hard sell and swell as the radio spot ends. Another bonus to working in this multitrack environment is that you can combine mono voice recordings with stereo sound effects and music in the final mix. That's just some of the power you have with a multitrack software program. And while you can do the same thing in an audio editor, it's much easier to do it with this kind of specialized software instead.

Multitrack software lets you record, edit, sweeten, mix, and deliver a final audio segment. If you want you can choose to record all your separate sound elements using an audio editor such as the Sound Forge software, and then switch to the multitrack to build and mix the final piece. This is the way Adobe Audition works, combining a mono/stereo recorder/editor with multitrack functionality!

Multitrack software is usually non-destructive, which means any edits you make do not physically affect the sound files. The software keeps track of the changes and applies them in real time. This means you must take an extra step to render, or save, the completed piece to the file format(s) you need (.wav, MP3, .aiff, and so on). The great thing is that if you make a mistake, you can go back and remix without losing any of your original audio.

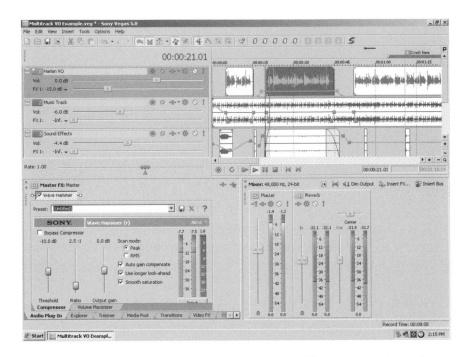

Sony Vegas is multitrack software for the PC and is ideal for more complex audio projects.

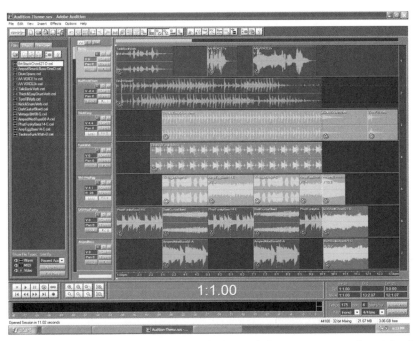

Multitrack software lets you keep individual sound elements separated until the final mix for more creative control.

Multitrack software is also ideal for putting together your demo. After you get all your spots into your computer, use the software to edit, rearrange, and mix a killer demo sequence. Then you can render it as a final .wav file suitable for burning CDs, or make MP3s for your Web site or your agent's. Using the Vegas software, you can burn CDs from within the program. Sweet.

Finishing Secrets

You've edited your voice files and sweetened them in ways that make sense for the project. Once you're happy with the recording, save it with a project name and add the extension "master" to the file, as in "AGHR Voice Intro MASTER.wav." Make this master the highest-quality digital file you can. In other words, if you recorded at CD quality, 16 bit, 44.1 kHz, save it to that format.

Use this master to create any other file formats you need. For example, if the producer wants you to e-mail an MP3, create it from this master version. See Chapter 7 for details on preparing your files for the Web, including the MP3 format. If the producer wants the file on CD, simply burn the CD from this master file.

Burn Baby Burn

The basic process of making CDs uses a laser to burn information onto a die-coated plastic disc. You can make two different kinds of CDs in a CD-R/CD-RW/DVD writer—audio and data. Many computers today have DVD burners that also can make CDs. Rarely, if ever, would you make a DVD for a client or audition.

Burning an audio CD creates a disc that can play on virtually any home or car CD player. A data CD, or CD-ROM, is simply a storage device, no different than a floppy disk or hard drive that can be accessed on a computer. Data CDs *do not* play on audio CD players, only computers. Make sure you clearly tell your client whether the CD is audio or data. Harlan and Jeffrey can recount several panicky calls from clients who didn't realize the data disc they'd requested wouldn't play on a CD player!

Some producers might want an audio CD, while others might prefer just the data CD with the finished .wav file on it. The latter may simply import your voice recording into the software he or she uses to create the finished spot. For example, a video producer might use a computer to edit the production, and can simply slip in your narration along with production audio.

There are several software utilities for burning both data and audio CDs. Chances are one shipped with your computer if it was equipped with a CD-R/CD-RW writer. Popular choices include Easy CD Creator (http://www.roxio.com), Nero (http://www.nero.com), and RecordNow (http://www.sonic.com). The software is typically easy to use. You simply drag and drop the files you want to the program, slip a blank CD-R into the drive, and click on Record. Slightly more advanced and more expensive versions of CD burner software will allow you to create a mixed-mode or CD-extra that can contain both data and audio on the same disc.

The Audition, Sound Forge, and Vegas applications all include burning CDs as part of their functions. Using one of these applications means you don't have to buy another software product, and that saves times and money.

By the way, always use blank CD-Rs for making CDs, not CD-RWs. Often CD-RWs won't play on some players; you wouldn't want that, would you?

Always burn your CDs in what's called "disc at once" (DAO) mode. This essentially burns and closes the disc in one operation. If you use "track at once" mode you can add tracks over time, but until you close the disc it won't play anywhere except your computer.

To reduce errors and prevent otherwise ruined discs (called *coasters*), record at lower speeds. Just because you can burn at 24× the normal rate doesn't mean you should. Burn your most critical work at 1× speed. It takes longer, but the master CDs have fewer problems.

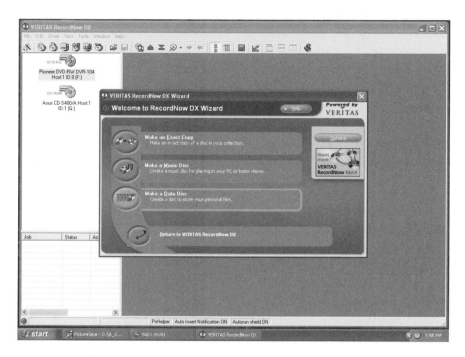

CD-burning software lets you make both audio and data CDs.

To burn an audio CD, your files must be 16 bit, 44.1 kHz, stereo. If you followed our advice and recorded in mono, you'll have to convert the file to stereo before burning an audio CD. If you just burn a data CD, you can ignore this step. In the Sound Forge application, choose Process > Channel Converter and then choose the preset mono to stereo, 50% faders option. The program will convert your mono file to a stereo file. It won't be real stereo; it's what's called dual mono—equal sound in both channels. The file will sound monaural, but the file format will conform to what the CD burner needs.

If you recorded at higher bit depths and sampling rates, you'll also need to use your audio editing software's bit depth converter and resample options to create CD-compatible files. When converting the bit depth, say from 24 to 16 bits, you'll want to apply some dither. Without moving to absolute geek central, let's just say that dither makes the conversion sound better. Dither adds a little noise to the file to mask the effects of quantization noise that result when you lower the bit depth. Okay, we said we wouldn't go there. Sorry, we just got carried away—you know, in a dither.

Video Production, Too

You can work with video the same way you do audio in your own home studio. Video work requires some additional hardware, specialized software, and a relatively robust computer to be viable. If you need to compile a video demo reel of your onscreen/onstage work or audition for screen or stage projects, this might be the best, least expensive route, and later you can finally take all those old eight, super eight, and home video tapes in the sock drawer, edit out the boring parts—usually 99 percent of the footage—and make DVDs for the whole family!

For video work you need a fast computer with an equally large (60 GB) and fast hard drive (7200 rpm) and a digital IE-1394 port, sometimes called a FireWire port. You also need a Mini Digital Video (DV) camcorder. Although there are devices that can convert analog video signals, such as VHS tapes, to the DV format, a camcorder is often the better choice. The camcorder will do the conversion for you, and you can use it to videotape auditions or for other needs. For example, this setup is perfect for independent filmmaking or other personal videos.

You can use a computer-based video editor to build video demo reels.

If you have analog video of your performances, say on VHS tape, you simply connect the output of any home VHS player to the input of the Mini-DV camcorder and record with it. This step converts the analog video to digital video. Next, you plug the DV camcorder into the computer using the special IE-1394 port. You then use software on the computer to transfer the files from the DV camcorder to the computer, in a process called *video capture*.

Once the digital video is on the computer, you use specialized video software to edit the video as needed. You can shorten sequences, add titles, and get creative with the tools provided by the software. Once you finish the editing, you render the file to a new DV file so you can copy it back to the camcorder and then onto new VHS tapes.

Alternatively, you can render the video to the popular Web formats. These files can be posted on the Net, e-mailed, or burned onto data CDs. You can also create DVD-compliant MPEGII files and make your own DVDs (if you have a DVD burner and software on your computer).

The Sony Media Software Vegas application combines feature-rich, broadcast-quality non-linear video editing (NLE) with a complete, powerful multitrack audio engine. You can use it for multitrack audio and/or video editing, and you can even burn audio CDs and video CDs (VCD) all from the program. This product is always getting new functionality, so it might do more by the time this book is printed.

9 } Dénouement: Our Last Act

Nightmare on West Meadowlark Lane

ACT TWO

STAGE LIGHTS FADE UP ON THE STILL PERFECTLY MODERN, PERFECTLY DECORATED, PERFECTLY EXPENSIVE KITCHEN OF GRIFF AND BETTE SMERSKY; IT IS SIX YEARS LATER. GRIFF, AS ALWAYS, IN BROOKS BROTHERS BUSINESS CASUAL, PERUSES THE *WALL STREET JOURNAL* AS BETTE BURSTS THROUGH SWINGING DOORS STAGE RIGHT, TALKING ON A WIRELESS PHONE AND SIPPING A STARBUCKS COFFEE IN A PAPER CUP. IT IS LATE AFTERNOON.

Bette: No, no, no, I ordered a café mocha double-shot espresso chai latté, no ephedrine. But there's only one shot in it—one shot! Hang on… (to Griff) Taste this.

Griff: One shot.

(HE HAS NOT LOOKED UP FROM THE PAPER.)

Bette: See? One shot! I expect a full refund and delivered to my door, young man.

(SHE CROSSES STAGE LEFT TO DUMP OUT THE COFFEE IN THE SINK AND GLANCES THROUGH THE WINDOW.)

Bette: Who do we know with a grey Audi TT convertible?

(HE PEERS OVER THE TOP OF THE PAPER.)

Griff: Maybe it's your refund from Starbucks?

(BETTE GIVES HIM A WITHERING LOOK.)

Bette: Oh my God, it's Johnny and…

Griff: And?

Bette: A woman, a girl, a quite attractive…

Griff: Really…

(JOHN, NOW AGE 24, BURSTS THROUGH THE SWINGING DOORS STAGE RIGHT.)

John: Heeeeeeeere's Johnny!

Bette: Honey!

(BETTE AIR-KISSES HIM WHILE SIMULTANEOUSLY WIPING A SMUDGE OFF THE STAINLESS STEEL SIDE-BY-SIDE REFRIGERATOR.)

John: And heeeeeeeeere's Kim, my…

(HE PAUSES MELODRAMATICALLY AS GRIFF AND BETTE LEAN FORWARD.)

John: (Continued) Really good friend…

(GRIFF AND BETTE LEAN BACK, RELIEVED.)

John: …and my wife!

Bette: Ohmygod!

(BETTE SWOONS AGAINST THE HAND-CARVED GRANITE COUNTERTOP.)

Griff: Now look what you've done.

(BETTE CROSSES UPSTAGE, STEADIES HERSELF AT THE STAINLESS STEEL COMMERCIAL STOVE, THEN LUNGES FOR THE REFRIGERATOR AND PULLS A WATER BOTTLE FROM WITHIN. SHE GULPS A SWIG WHILE CROSSING DOWNSTAGE AND TOSSES IT TO GRIFF, WHO SNATCHES IT FROM THE AIR WITH ONE HAND. BETTE CRADLES JOHN'S HEAD BETWEEN HER HANDS.)

Bette: Johnny, you're an…an actor. They're paying you what, maybe a couple thousand dollars a week to traipse across the hinterlands singing your heart out, five shows a week as that Che character….

John: Six hundred dollars, nine shows a week, but who's counting? I'm happy and I have…

(HE LOOKS AT KIM.)

Griff: (Getting up and crossing to his new daughter-in-law and finishing John's sentence.) …Kim, is it? Welcome to the family.

THEY SHAKE HANDS AWKWARDLY.

Guess that's your car out there?

Kim: Actually it's John's. I drive an old beat-up Toyota; it's the best I can afford.

Griff: As an actress?

Kim: As a junior associate attorney, Mr. Smersky. I'm sure you remember what it was like starting out: the pay sucks, the hours are horrendous, the competition between associates is disgustingly fierce, and I'll be paying back school loans forever.

Life is all too often way too short. Since we all spend so much of our lives working, we'd all love to make our living doing what we love. Unfortunately, most people have to sell their dreams short because of the realities of life—we need to earn a living, pay the rent, educate our kids, pay off our school loans, and meet any number of life's demands. Even people like Kim, who have chosen a "regular" career with a pretty clear-cut career path, struggle with life's never-ending financial obligations.

You, on the other hand, have made a giant leap of faith by choosing to make your way in the world as an actor. We salute you for actually having the courage to do what you love and hoping, often against all hope, to make your living at it.

Young attorney-to-be Kim, after working hard for low pay for a few years, will most likely earn a hefty salary. Eventually that will skyrocket when she becomes a partner in the law firm. At retirement age, she will become "of counsel" and go relax on her 50-acre estate in New Mexico. You will most likely struggle paying the bills until the day you die, unless you hit it big and become a lifelong celebrity.

That's where your voiceover work can really pay off. Some of us choose to make voice work our entire acting career. Others see voice work as a way to pay the bills while pursuing the stage or screen. Whichever direction you choose, performing voiceovers is not only fun, it's frequently remunerative if—and that's a big *if*—you follow our advice. In addition to developing your voice acting skills, snaring a top voice agent, and creating marketable demos and a Web site of your own, you'll need a career-long commitment to self-promotion. You'll also need to equip yourself with recording equipment and the knowledge you need to use it. And now that you've finished our book, you should possess the basic skills you need to succeed.

You've learned how to set up a home-based (even portable) studio of your own. You've seen how it can save you time and money and perhaps even make you some extra cash to boot. Hopefully, your new knowledge of recording and editing audio, along with an increased awareness of proper microphone placement and techniques, has already made you a better voiceover performer as well. Best of all, with a good phone patch (or better yet, ISDN capability in your studio), you can now compete worldwide.

Join Us Online

We realize, of course, that recording skills, technology, and equipment are constantly changing. You'll need to continue learning this art, just as you continue to study the art of acting. To help, we've established a Web site just for actors with home recording studios: Audio Smart Actors (http://www.audiosmartactors.com). Here you'll find the latest information about today's recording and Internet technology. Think of it as a continual update to this book. It's the smart way to stay informed and educated about ways to make your voiceover career better. We hope you'll join us there often.

By now you know a simple truth: You absolutely *can* set up and run your own personal recording studio. And we know a simple truth: If you build it, they *will* come!

Before we go, one little last bit of business—the finale, the dénouement, the ending, when our favorite parent-figures, Griff and Bette Smersky, have to come to grips with reality—and their son—the successful voiceover....

Griff and Bette: John, how can you afford to get married and buy a convertible as an actor?

John: It's peanuts, Dad and Mom.

Bette: Peanuts! Supporting a wife and…

(SHE STUDIES KIM'S VERY FLAT STOMACH.)

(CONTINUES)

…a family someday is peanuts to you! Griff, call Rudy, tell him I cannot work out today or for the foreseeable future. We…we have another family crisis.

John: Mom, Dad, I auditioned for the voice of Mr. Peanut and got cast in six network TV commercials. Then I did four Audi voiceover commercials—figured the least I could do in return was buy one of their cars! Look, I'm really busy. In fact we've bought some home studio recording equipment that's also portable and now I can earn money anywhere in the world! Anywhere there's an Internet connection, a production of *Evita*, and, of course, Kim!

(KIM AND JOHN HUG. BETTE SMILES WANLY AT GRIFF, WHO NODS, SHAKES JOHN'S, KIM'S, AND BETTE'S HANDS, AND THEN SITS DOWN TO READ HIS *WALL STREET JOURNAL*.)

THE END

CURTAIN

Resources

Books by Your Authors

Fisher, Jeffrey P. *Instant Sound Forge*
(San Francisco: CMP Books, 2004)

Fisher, Jeffrey P. *Profiting from Your Music and Sound Project Studio*
(New York: Allworth Press, 2001)

Fisher, Jeffrey P. *Ruthless Self-Promotion in the Music Industry*
(Vallejo: ArtistPro, 1999)

Hogan, Harlan. *VO: Tales and Techniques of a Voiceover Actor*
(New York: Allworth Press, 2002)

Other Helpful Books

Levinson, Jay Conrad and Seth Godin. *The Guerrilla Marketing Handbook*
(New York: Houghton Mifflin, 1995)

Long, Ben. *Making Digital Videos*
(Hingham, MA: Charles River Media, 2002)

Rose, Jay. *Audio Postproduction for Digital Video*
(Manhasset, NY: CMP Books, 2002)

Periodicals

Backstage, Backstage West, and
Backstage Handbook for the Performing Artist
1515 Broadway, 14th Floor
New York, NY 10035
http://www.backstage.com

Hollywood Reporter
5055 Wilshire Boulevard
Los Angeles, CA 90036
http://www.hollywoodreporter.com

PerformInk
3223 N. Sheffield, 3rd Floor
Chicago, IL 60657
http://www.performink.com

Ross Reports (monthly)
770 Broadway, 4th Floor
New York, NY 10003
http://www.backstage.com/backstage/rossreports/index.jsp

Screen Magazine
222 West Ontario Street Suite 500
Chicago, IL 60610
http://www.screenmag.tv

Variety
5700 Wilshire Boulevard
Los Angeles, CA 90036
http://www.variety.com

Voice Over Resource Guide
Dave & Dave Inc.
4352 Lankershim Boulevard
Toluca Lake, CA 91602
http://www.voiceoverresourceguide.com

EQ Magazine
CMP United Media
Music Player Network
2800 Campus Drive
San Mateo, CA 94403
http://www.eqmag.com

Mix Magazine
PO Box 1939
Marion, OH 43306
http://www.mixonline.com

Electronic Musician Magazine
PO Box 1929
Marion, OH 43306
http://www.emusician.com

Recording Software

Adobe Audition (Windows computers only)
Adobe Systems Incorporated
345 Park Avenue
San Jose, CA 95110-2704
http://www.adobe.com/products/audition/main.html

Sound Forge, Vegas, and ACID (Windows computers only)
Sony Pictures Digital, Inc.
Media Software and Services
1617 Sherman Avenue
Madison, WI 53704
http://www.sony.com/mediasoftware

Pro Tools
Digidesign, a division of Avid Technology, Inc.
2001 Junipero Serra Blvd.
Daly City, CA 94014-3886
http://www.digidesign.com

Tracktion
Mackie
16220 Wood-Red Road N.E.
Woodinville, WA 98072
http://www.mackie.com

Audacity
http://audacity.sourceforge.net

BIAS Peak (Macintosh computers only)
BIAS, Inc.
1370 Industrial Avenue, Suite A
Petaluma, CA, 94952
http://www.bias-inc.com

Recording Equipment and Supplies

B&H Pro Audio
420 Ninth Avenue
New York, NY 10001
http://www.bhphotovideo.com

Full Compass
8001 Terrace Avenue
Middleton, WI 53562
http://www.fullcompass.com

Markertek Supply
812 Kings Highway
PO Box 397
Saugerties, NY 12477
http://www.markertek.com

Sweetwater
5335 Bass Road
Fort Wayne, IN 46808
http://www.sweetwater.com

Musician's Friend
PO Box 4370
Medford, OR 97501
http://www.musiciansfriend.com

BSW
Broadcast Supply Worldwide
7012 27th Street West
Tacoma, WA 98466
http://www.bswusa.com

American Musical Supply
P.O. Box 152
Spicer, MN 56288
http://www.americanmusical.com

Guitar Center
5795 Lindero Canyon Road
Westlake Village, CA 91362
http://www.guitarcenter.com

Sam Ash
http://www.samash.com/home

ISDN

Digifon ISDN Services
20 Deep Wood Road
Fairfield, CT 06430
http://www.digifon.com

Ednet
200 Vallejo Street
San Francisco, CA 94111
http://www.ednet.net

Phone Patch

CircuitWerkes
2805 NW 6th Street
Gainesville, FL 32609
http://www.broadcastboxes.com/images/harlan

Acoustic Material

Acoustics First
2247 Tomlynn Street
Richmond, VA 23230
http://www.acousticsfirst.com

Auralex Acoustics
6853 Hillsdale Court
Indianapolis, IN 46250
http://www.auralex.com

Silent
58 Nonotuck Street
Northampton, MA 01062
http://www.silentsource.com

Sound Booths

VocalBooth
1631 SE Riviera Drive
Bend, OR 97702
http://www.vocalbooth.com

WhisperRoom
116 S. Sugar Hollow Road
Morristown, TN 37813
http://www.whisperroom.com

Web Resources

Webmaster Warren King
FlowTech Solutions, Inc
11 Crowley Court
Raymond, NH 03077-1551
603-895-0964
wking@flowtech-solutions.com

Domain registration
Network Solutions, Inc.
Herndon, VA
http://www.networksolutions.com

Web site hosting
ADDR.com, Inc.
560 S. Winchester Blvd., Floor 5
San Jose, CA 95128
http://www.addr.com

Authors' Contact Information

Jeffrey P. Fisher can be reached via e-mail or through his Web site.
E-mail: jpf@jeffreypfisher.com
Web: http://www.jeffreypfisher.com

Harlan Hogan can be reached via e-mail, through his agents, or on the Web.
E-mail: Harlan@HarlanHogan.com
Web: http://www.HarlanHogan.com

Agents:

Access Talent
37 East 28th Street, Suite 500
New York, NY 10016
(212) 684–7795
http://www.accesstalent.com

Stewart Talent
58 West Huron
Chicago, IL 60610
(312) 943–3131
http://www.stewarttalent.com

William Morris Agency
One William Morris Place
Beverly Hills, CA 90212
(310) 859–4000
http://www.wma.com

Richard Hutchinson Management
3071 Arden Rd.
Atlanta, GA 30305
404-403-8447
http://www.rshmanagement.com

DB Talent
7402 Brodie Lane
Austin, TX 78745-5834
512-292-1030
http://www.dbtalent.com

Lori Lins Ltd
7611 W. Holmes Ave.
Milwaukee, WI 53220
414-282-3500
http://www.lorilins.com

Web:

http://www.StudioCenter.com (Norfolk)

http://www.SoundOfTheWeb.net (London)

http://www.intervoice.nl (Netherlands)

http://www.commercialvoices.com (Canada)

Index

A

Access Talent Web site, 156
accounting software, 14
ACID software, 136–137, 153
acoustics
    acoustic energy, 18
    acoustic material, resources, 157–158
    Acoustics First Web site, 157
active monitors, 33–34
Actor Track program, 13
ADC (analog-to-digital converter), 18
ADDR Web site, 102
address books, PDAs, 13
address naming considerations, e-mail, 15
Adobe Audition recording software, 31, 153
advertising, as promotion technique, 84–85, 94
agents, audio sites, 99
AKG C414 microphones, 23
Alesis M1 Active Studio monitors, 34
ambient sound effects, 134
American Musical Supply Web site, 157
analog recording, 18
analog-to-digital converter (ADC), 18
APT (Audio Processing Technology), 78–79
archives, 62–63
attack settings
    noise gates, 121
    volume inconsistencies, 126–127
Audacity recording software, 153
audio
    audio quality, telephone phone patch disadvantages, 74
    audio sites, 99–100
    extracting from CDs, 138
    interface preamps, 29–30
Audio Postproduction for Digital Video (Jay Rose), 152
Audio Processing Technology (ADT), 78–79
Audio Smart Actors Web site, 101, 150
Audiobahn Web site, 77
AudioTX Web site, 80

Audition software (Adobe), 31, 153
auditioning
    phone patches, 6
    soliciting business, 4–6
    via e-mail, 102
Auralex Web site, 40, 158
author contact information, 156–157

B
background noises. *See* noise interference
background sound effects, 134
Backstage, Backstage West, and Backstage Handbook for the Performing Artist, 152
backups, 62–63
banner ads, as promotion technique, 91
basements, as home recording studio, 34
bedrooms, as home recording studio, 34
Behringer B2031 Truth monitor, 34
B&H Pro Audio Web site, 155
BIAS Peak software, 32, 155
Big Fish Audio Web site, 137
bit depth, 18
books, resources, 152
booths, recording, 38–39
breathing sounds
    correcting, 119
    microphone use, 66
Broadcast ISDN User Guide & Directory Web site, 77
Broadcast Supply Worldwide (BSW) Web site, 71, 155
bulletin boards, as promotion techniques, 94
burning CDs, 141–145
business, soliciting. *See also* promotion techniques
    auditioning, 4–6
    demos, 6–7
    Internet options, 7–8
    lingo, talking the talk, 8
    lower budget solutions, 8
business cards, as promotion technique, 90

C
cable modems, Internet connections, 15
cable selection, microphones, 25

calendars, PDAs, 14

cardioid microphones, 20–21

cases, microphone, 26

catch breaths, 66

CDs

    burning, 141–145

    demos, soliciting business through, 7–8

    extracting audio from, 138

    purchasing considerations, 12

Central Processing Unit (CPU), 11

CircuitWerkes Web site, 157

clicking noises, 128

clip restoration utility, 131–132

clipboard, 68

coasters, 142

codec (code/decode), 73

commands, basic editing, 67

CommercialVoices Web site, 159

compression formats

    extreme compression, 130

    lossy, 108

computer-based recording program, 2–3

computer systems

    CPU (Central Processing Unit), 11

    flexibility considerations, 9

    GB (gigabytes), 11

    hardware issues, 11–13

    Internet connections, 14–16

    keyboards, 11

    Mac-based software, 10

    memory issues, 11

    monitor selection, 13

    monitors, 11

    mouse, 11

    PC-based software, 10

    printer selection, 13

    purchasing considerations, 10–11

    reasons for, 9

    software issues, 13–14

    soundcards, 11

    speed considerations, 9

condenser microphones, 19–20

connections, Internet, 14–16

contact management systems, 13

Contour Design ShuttlePRO V2, 12

copies, demos, 87

copying, editing basics, 67

cord selection, microphones, 25

corrections. *See* problems, correcting

CPU (Central Processing Unit), 11

cutting, editing basics, 67–68

D

DAO (disc at once) mode, 142

DB Talent Web site, 159

DC offset, 124

deleting, editing basics, 67

delivery delay, telephone phone patch disadvantages, 74

demos

    CD options, 7–8

    copies, 87

    Internet options, 7–8

    length considerations, 88

    as promotion technique, 85–86

    rough cut, 7

    soliciting business, 6–7

    structure considerations, 86

denture noises, 119

desks, home recording studio setup, 35

dial-up connections, 14, 75–76

Digifon Web site, 157

digital recording software, 30–32

direct contact, as promotion technique, 84

direct mail, as promotion technique, 91–92

direct response, as promotion technique, 84

disc at once (DAO) mode, 142

Disc Makers Web site, 98

distortion, 53, 55

domain names, 100–101

Domain registration Web resource, 158

downloading *versus* streaming, 110

driver installations, production procedures, 42

DSL lines, Internet connections, 15
dull recording, 129
dynamic microphones, 19–20

E
e-mail
    address name considerations, 15
    sending auditions via, 102
Easy CD Creator software, 142
echo sound effects, 133
editing basics
    basic computer commands, 67
    copying, 67
    cutting, 67–68
    deleting, 67
    markers, inserting, 69
    overview, 66
    pasting, 67
    pre-editing preparation, 63–66
    selecting, 67
    trimming, 67
    waveform selections, 67
editors, sound, 30
Ednet Web site, 157
effects. *See* sound effects
Electro-Voice RE20 microphones, 23
Electronic Musician Magazine, 153
encoding
    file preparation, 110–115
    normalization tools, 112–113
EQ (equalization)
    extraneous noises, 120
    telephone sound effects, 132
    Web encoding file preparation, 110–111
EQ Magazine, 153
equipment and supplies, resources, 155–156
errors. *See* problems, correcting
Event's 20/20bas V2 monitor, 34
Everything VO Web site, 46
extraneous noises, 119–120
extreme compression, 130

F

fades, 124–125

feedback, microphone use, 44

female voices

microphone selection for, 24–25, 56

pitch-shifting effects, 133–134

file name considerations, folder creation, 62

file preparation, encoding, 110–115

File Transfer Protocol (FTP), 102–103

files, saving, 62

FirstCom Music Web site, 136

Fisher, Jeffrey P.

contact information, 156

Instant Sound Forge, 152

Profiting from Your Music and Sound Project Studio, 152

Ruthless Self-Promotion in the Music Industry, 152

flexibility considerations, computer systems, 9

FlowTech Solutions Web site, 158

folder creation, 62

Fresh Music Web site, 136

FTP (File Transfer Protocol), 102–103

Full Compass Web site, 155

G

GB (gigabytes), 11

Godin, Seth *(The Guerrilla Marketing Handbook),* 94, 152

GoldWave software, 30

ground lifts, 123

Guerrilla Marketing Handbook, The (Jay Conrad Levinson and Seth Godin), 94, 152

Guitar Center Web site, 157

H

hard sound effects, 134

hardware issues, computer systems, 11–13

headphones, selection considerations, 33

headset, phone patches and, 71

help options, promotion techniques, 94–95

hissing and humming sounds, 123–124

Hogan, Harlan

contact information, 156

VO: Tales and Techniques of a Voice-Over Actor, 89, 91, 152

Hollywood Edge Web site, 135
Hollywood Reporter, 153
home recording. *See* recording
HTML (Hypertext Markup Language), 103
humming and hissing sounds, 123–124

I
iBuilder company, 92
independents, audio sites, 99
Instant Sound Forge (Jeffrey P. Fisher), 152
interfaces, phone patches, 71–72
Internet
    audio sites, 99–100
    connections, 14–16
    domain names, 100–101
    encoding
        file preparation, 110–115
        normalization tools, 112–113
    MP3 format, 109
    phone patches, 80–81
    as promotion technique, 92
    Real Media format, 109
    soliciting business through, 7–8
    streaming *versus* downloading, 110
    virtual voiceover, 115–116
    voiceover actors and, 97–98
    Web design
        do-it-yourself, 103–104
        professional, 105
    Web hosting
        dedicated, 101–103
        voiceover readiness, 108–109
    Windows Media format, 109
Intervoice Web site, 159
ISDN
    Internet connections, 15
    phone patches
        advantages of, 75–76
        dial-up setup, 75–76
        dropping lines, 81–82
        installations, 78

resources, 157

K

keyboards, computer systems, 11
Keyspan Digital Media Remote Web site, 12
Killer Tracks Web site, 136
King, Warren, 105–108

L

legal concerns, promotion techniques, 95
length considerations, demos, 88
Levinson, Jay Conrad *(The Guerrilla Marketing Handbook)*, 94, 152
libraries, music, 136
limiting, 130
line-level signals, preamps, 27
lingo considerations, soliciting business, 8
lip smack noises, 117–118
logistic concerns, promotion techniques, 95
Long, Ben *(Making Digital Videos)*, 152
loops, 136–137
Lori Lins Ltd Web site, 159
lossy compression format, 108
loud files, 129–130
low-budget solutions, soliciting business, 8

M

M-Audio BX5 monitors, 34
Mac-based software, 10
Mackie Spike audio interface, 31
mailings, as promotion technique, 91–92
Making Digital Video (Ben Long), 152
male voices
    microphone selection for, 24–25
    pitch shifting effects, 133–134
markers, inserting, editing basics, 69
Markertek Supply Web site, 39, 155
Marshall MXL 2001/2003 microphones, 23
Masterbits Web site, 137
Media Software (Sony), 30
Melomania Web site, 136
memory issues, computer systems, 11

memos, PDAs, 14
microphones
    AKG C414, 23
    breathing in, 66
    cable selection, 25
    cardioid, 20–21
    caring for, 26
    cases for, 26
    condenser, 19–20
    cord selections, 25
    costs, 19, 23–24
    dynamic, 19–20
    Electro-Voice RE20, 23
    feedback, 44
    female voice considerations, 24–25, 56
    how to use, 45
    male voice considerations, 24–25
    Marshall MXL 2001/2003, 23
    moving coil, 19
    Neumann TLM 23, 103
    noise interference, 55
    omnidirectional, 20
    optimal recording levels, 44–45
    pickup patterns, 20
    positioning considerations, 55–56
    preamps, 27–30
    production procedures, 43
    proper miking example, 56–57
    proximity effect, 21
    Rode NT1-A, 23
    selection considerations, 24–25
    Sennheiser MD 421, 23
    shotgun, 20–21
    Shure KSM27, 23
    Shure SM57/SM58, 23
    sibilance, 57–58
    side miking example, 56–57
    unidirectional, 20
Microsoft Money accounting software, 14
MicTel interface, phone patches, 71
miking. *See* microphones

mistakes. *See* problems, correcting

Mix Magazine, 153

mix minus requirements, phone patches, 72

mixers, 27–28

Modern Postcard Web site, 91

monitors. *See also* speakers

    active, 33–34

    computer systems, selection considerations, 11, 13

    passive, 33

    powered, 34

    types of, 34

Motion Picture Experts Group (MPEG), 78–79

mouse, computer systems, 11

moving coil microphones, 19

MP3 format, 109

MPEG (Motion Picture Experts Group), 78–79

multitrack systems, 30–31, 138–141

music

    loops, 136–137

    Music Bakery Web site, 136

    music libraries, 136

Musician's Friend Web site, 155

N

n-Track tool, 31

Nero Web site, 142

Network Solutions Web site, 101, 158

Neumann TLM 103 microphones, 23

niche market, 115

noise interference

    breathing sounds, 119

    clicking noises, 128

    denture noises, 119

    extraneous noises, 119–120

    general background noises, 121–123

    home studio setup, 36

    humming or hissing, 123–124

    lip smacks, 117–118

    microphone placement, 55

    noise gates, 121–123

    plosives, 131

thin sounds, 128
normalization tools, encoding, 112–113
Norman, Marc, 1

O
omnidirectional microphones, 20
Omnimusic Web site, 136
output control, volume inconsistencies, 127

P
Pair Networks Web site, 102
passive monitors, 33
pasting, editing basics, 67
patches, phone patches
    Internet options, 80–81
    ISDN phone patches
        advantages of, 75–76
        dial-up setup, 75–76
        dropping lines, 81–82
        installations, 78
    resources, 157
    telephone phone patches
        auditioning, 6
        disadvantages of, 74–75
        headsets, 71
        interfaces, 71–72
        MicTel interface, 71
        mix minus requirements, 72
        POTS line, 70
        XLR connectors, 71
PC-based software, 10
PDAs (Personal Digital Assistant), 13
peak normalization, 112
PerformInk, 153
periodicals, 152–154
Personal Digital Assistant (PDAs), 13
Personal Information Manager (PIM), 13
phantom power, mixers, 27
phasing, 130
phone lines, dial-up connections, 14
phone patches

Internet options, 80–81
ISDN phone patches
   advantages of, 75–76
   dial-up setup, 75–76
   dropping lines, 81–82
   installations, 78
resources, 157
telephone phone patches
   auditioning, 6
   disadvantages of, 74–75
   headsets, 71
   interfaces, 71–72
   MicTel interface, 71
   mix minus requirements, 72
   POTS line, 70
   XLR connectors, 71
pickup patterns, microphones, 20
PIM (Personal Information Manager), 13
pitch shifting sound effects, 133–134
plosives, 131
plug-ins, 115
pop filters, 25–26
postcards, as promotion technique, 90
POTS line, phone patches, 70
powered monitors, 34
preamps
   audio interface, 29–30
   levels, setting, 46
   microphones, 27–30
   mixers, 27–28
   stand-alone, 28–29
   volume control, 46–47
printers, selection considerations, 13
Pro Tools, 31, 153
problems, correcting
   bad edits, 124
   breathing sounds, 119
   clicking noises, 128
   clip restoration utility, 131–132
   denture noises, 119
   dull recording, 129

extraneous noises, 119–120
fades, 124–125
general background noises, 121–123
ground lifts, 123
humming or hissing, 123–124
lip smacks, 117–118
loud files, 129–130
plosives, 131
sentence pickups, 125
sibilance, 131
thin sounds, 128
timing issues, 130
volume inconsistencies, 125–127
production procedures
driver installations, 42
microphone placement, 55–56
reflective sound considerations, 43
sound booth setup, 43
volume control, 55
professional Web design, 105
Profiting from Your Music and Sound Project Studio (Jeffrey P. Fisher), 95, 152
promotion techniques. *See also* soliciting business
advertising, 84–85, 94
banner ads, 91
bulletin boards, 94
considerations, 92–93
demos, 85–86, 88
direct contact, 84
direct mail, 91–92
direct response, 84
help options, 94–95
Internet direct mail, 92
legal and logistic concerns, 95
to other actors, 93–94
printed promotions, 94
promotional blurbs, 90
publicity, 84
Web promotion, 91
proximity effect, 21
publicity, as promotion technique, 84
purchasing considerations

CDs, 12
computer systems, 10–11

Q
Q Up Arts Web site, 137
quality considerations, computer systems, 9
quantizing, 18
Quicken accounting software, 14

R
RAM (random access memory), 11–12
ratio settings, volume inconsistencies, 126
Real Media format, 109
recording
    analog, 18
    booths, 38–39
    computer-based program, 2–3
    computer systems
        flexibility considerations, 9
        hardware issues, 11–13
        Internet connections, 14–16
        Mac-based software, 10
        memory issues, 11
        monitor selection, 13
        PC-based software, 10
        printer selection, 13
        purchasing considerations, 10–11
        reasons for, 9–10
        software issues, 13–14
        speed considerations, 9
    digital recording software, 30–32
    dull, 129
    good recording levels, 52
    overview, 17
    pop filters, 25–26
    sample script, 59–61
    software resources, 154–155
    studio setup, 34–37
    tracking, 58–63
RecordNow software, 142
reflective sound considerations, production procedures, 43

release
    noise gates, 121
    volume inconsistencies, 126–127
resources
    acoustic material, 157–158
    author contact information, 156–157
    books, 152
    equipment and supplies, 155–156
    ISDN, 157
    music libraries, 136
    periodicals, 152–154
    phone patch, 157
    recording software, 154–155
    sound booths, 158
    sound effects, 135
    Web, 158–159
responsibility, telephone phone patch disadvantages, 74–75
reverberation effects, 132
Richard Hutchinson Management Web site, 159
RMS normalization, 112
Rode NT1-A microphones, 23
Roland MA8 Micro monitors, 34
room setup, home recording, 34–37
Rose, Jay (*Audio Postproduction for Digital Video*), 152
Ross Reports, 153
rough-cut demos, 7
Ruthless Self-Promotion in the Music Industry (Jeffrey P. Fisher), 95, 152

S
Sam Ash Web site, 157
sample recording script, 59–61
sampling, 18
sampling rates, 18, 142
saving files, 62
Screen Magazine, 153
selecting, editing basics, 67
Sennheiser MD 421 microphone, 23
sentence pickups, 125
service providers, Internet connections, 14
shotgun microphones, 20–21
ShowBiz Web site, 99

Shure KSM27 microphones, 23
Shure SM57/SM58 microphones, 23
Shure Web site, 23
sibilance
    controlling, 131
    microphone use, 57–58
side miking example, 56–57
Silent Web site, 158
sites. *See* Web sites
soft sound effects, 134
software
    accounting, 14
    ACID, 136–137, 153
    contact management systems, 13
    digital recording, 30–32
    Easy CD Creator, 142
    RecordNow, 142
    software issues, computer systems, 13–14
    Sound Forge, 138, 153
soliciting business. *See also* promotion techniques
    auditioning, 4–6
    demos, 6–7
    Internet options, 7–8
    lingo, talking the talk, 8
    lower-budget solutions, 8
SONEX Web site, 40
Sonic Spot Web site, 31
Sonomic Web site, 135, 137
Sony Media Software Sound Forge Audio Studio, 30–31
sound
    acoustic energy, 18
    reflective sound considerations, production procedures, 43
    vibration, 18
sound booths
    resources, 158
    setting up, production procedures, 43
sound editors, 30
sound effects
    adding, 138
    ambient effects, 134
    background, 134

echoes, 133
hard effects, 134
pitch shifting, 133–134
purchasing, 135
resources, 135
reverberation, 132
soft effects, 134
source music, 135
swirlies, 133
telephone sounds, 132
underscore, 135
Sound Effects Library Web site, 135
Sound Forge software, 138, 153
Sound Ideas of America Web site, 135
soundcards, 11
SoundDogs Web site, 135
SoundOfTheWeb Web site, 159
source music, 135
speakers. *See also* monitors
positioning, 35
selection considerations, 32–33
speed considerations, computer systems, 9
stand-alone preamps, 28–29
Stewart Talent Web site, 156
Stoppard, Tom, 1
streaming *versus* downloading, 110
studio setup, recording, 34–37
StudioCenter Web site, 159
supplies and equipment, resources, 155–156
Sweetwater Web site, 155
swirlie sound effects, 133

T
telephone phone patches
auditioning, 6
disadvantages of, 74–75
headsets, 71
interfaces, 71–72
MicTel interface, 71
mix minus requirements, 72
POTS line, 70

XLR connectors, 71
telephone sound effects, 132
The Guerrilla Marketing Handbook (Jay Conrad Levinson and Seth Godin), 94, 152
thin sounds, correcting, 128
threshold
    noise gates, 121
    volume inconsistencies, 126
timing issues, correcting, 130
to-do lists, PDAs, 13–14
Tracktion software, 31, 153
trimming, editing basics, 67

U
underscore, 135
unidirectional microphones, 20

V
Variety, 153
Vegas software, 153
vibration, 17
VideoHelper Web site, 136
virtual voiceover, 115–116
Vista Print Web site, 91
VO: Tales and Techniques of a Voice-Over Actor (Harlan Hogan), 89, 91, 152
VO boxes, 39–41
VocalBooth Web site, 37, 158
voice demos. *See* demos
Voice Over Resource Guide, 153
Voicebank Web site, 99
VoiceHunter Web site, 99
volume control
    distortion, 55
    inconsistencies, correcting, 125–127
    preamps, 46–47
    volume maximizer, 129
    VU meters, 55

W
Warren King Web resource, 158
Wave Hammer plug-in, 115
waveform selections, editing basics, 67

Web Hosting Ratings Web site, 102
Web promotion
    discussed, 91
    Web design
        do-it-yourself, 103–104
        professional, 105
    Web hosting
        dedicated, 101–103
        voiceover readiness, 108–109
Web resources, 158–159
Web sites
    Access Talent, 156
    ACIDPlanet, 137
    Acoustics First, 157
    ADDR, 102
    Alesis, 34
    American Musical Supply, 157
    audio sites, 99–100
    Audio Smart Actors, 101, 150
    Audiobahn, 77
    AudioTX, 80
    Auralex, 40, 158
    BIAS Peak, 32
    Big Fish Audio, 137
    Broadcast ISDN User Guide & Directory, 77
    Broadcast Supply Worldwide, 71, 155
    CommercialVoices, 159
    Contour Designs, 12
    DB Talent, 159
    Digifon, 157
    Disc Makers, 98
    Ednet, 157
    Everything VO, 46
    FirstCom Music, 136
    FlowTech Solutions, 158
    Fresh Music, 136
    GoldWave, 30
    Guitar Center, 157
    Hollywood Edge, 135
    Intervoice, 159
    Keyspan Digital Media Remote, 12

Killer Tracks, 136
Lori Lins Ltd, 159
Mackie, 31
Markertek, 39
Masterbits, 137
Melomania, 136
Modern Postcard, 91
Music Bakery, 136
n-Track, 31
Nero, 142
Network Solutions, 101, 158
Omnimusic, 136
Pair Networks, 102
Q Up Arts, 137
Richard Hutchinson Management, 159
Roland, 34
Sam Ash, 157
ShowBiz, 99
Shure, 23
Silent, 158
SONEX, 40
Sonic Spot, 31
Sonomic, 135, 137
Sound Effects Library, 135
Sound Ideas of America, 135
SoundDogs, 135
SoundOfTheWeb, 159
Stewart Talent, 156
StudioCenter, 159
VideoHelper, 136
Vista Print, 91
VocalBooth, 37, 158
voicebank, 99
VoiceHunter, 99
Web Hosting, 102
Whisper Room, 37
WhisperRoom, 158
William Morrison Agency, 156
Whisper Room Web site, 37, 158
William Morris Agency Web site, 156
Windows Media format, 109

WYSIWYG (What You *See* Is What You Get), 104

X
XLR connectors, phone patches, 71
Xpress software (ACID), 137